You Will
See Your Baby
In Heaven

A Man's Perspective of Stillbirth

You Will See Your Baby In Heaven

A Man's Perspective of Stillbirth

Drew Kelly *with* Mai Kelly

DREW KELLY PUBLISHING

DETROIT 2013

Published by Drew Kelly Publishing, Detroit, Michigan.

Library of Congress Cataloging-in-Publication Data

ISBN-13 978-0-9890757-0-1 (Hardcover)
ISBN-13 978-0-9890757-1-8 (Softcover)
ISBN-13 978-0-9890757-2-5 (eBook)

(CIP data applied for and to come)

Book typography and cover design by Norm Fletcher
Edited by Elizabeth Forsaith

Printed in the United States of America

FIRST EDITION

10 9 8 7 6 5 4 3 2 1

CONTENTS

Acknowledgments

My mother made a significant contribution toward making this publication possible in memory of my father, Scott Kelly, who passed away from cancer six months before this book was completed. Her hope is that this donation in his memory can help others in their time of loss.

Losing loved ones has to be one of the hardest realities in life.

Psalm 23 was one of the passages read at my father's funeral and serves as a good reminder of what we hope for in our walk with God. All losses of close family members whom you love are difficult.

Contributors

The following people were kind enough to support this writing. Without their financial contributions toward this project, it would not have happened. These kind souls understood the need for this story to be told to help others in a time of great distress. Mai and I are extremely grateful for all of their generous support.

Candace Kelly
Cody Kelly

Marilyn Roberts
Maria Teshuba
Ryan Whalen

Hugo Amorim
Kay and Jim Lynch
Dave & JoAnn Loewen

This book is dedicated to our son Reagan.
Your mother and I love and miss you so very, very much.
We can't wait to meet you in heaven.

Preface

Why Did I Write This Book?

Anyone who has lost a baby feels as if they should have died instead. They feel they are total failures as parents and don't deserve to live. I know that's how I felt. Several years ago my wife and I lost our unborn baby, who was almost at his due date, for no explainable medical reason. I want to share my story about how we managed to work through the pain and how we overcame this incredibly difficult life experience. I hope that by doing so I may be able to help someone who is struggling with a similar loss.

If you or someone you care about has experienced a stillbirth, my prayers are with you and your family during this tragic time. It never occurred to me to write a book about the loss of my second child until one of my coworkers experienced the same grief and loss in his family. After closing the office door, I talked with him about the sadness and recovery my wife, Mai, and I went through. I told him about how after our second child died we were able to have a happy life again and how we were able to go on and have a healthy baby. Our discussion and my suggestions for ways he could help his family left me walking away with very mixed feelings. Reliving the pain of losing a child was difficult, but the warm feeling of having helped another family was tremendous, and I knew there was a true purpose in that.

After thinking about it, it seemed to make sense that more people were hurting than I could possibly help in person. Sharing my story in this format is the most practical way to provide comfort to those in mourning. If this book helps provide any relief to you, or provides any help as you look for the answers to the hard questions for which there are no good answers right now, then I've achieved my goal in writing our story.

Mai has shared her feelings as honestly as possible to help you see both sides of our story. As time has passed, we've had flashbacks and time for recollection. The purpose of her words is to provide a wider perspective and to let you know how both of us felt at that time while trying to figure it out. Your wife may have a hard time expressing how she feels. She may be so overwhelmed that she doesn't even know all the feelings she's experiencing. Mai's shared feelings are not meant to be used to define what your wife's emotions are, but rather as an idea of what a woman who has been through this before felt during the tragic events while she was trying to navigate those challenges.

YOU WILL SEE YOUR BABY IN HEAVEN

1

What's My Story?

Our story is very painful to share. My wife and I wept a lot while writing this section, and it's not going to be easy to read. If you're hurting too much to read our story, you can skip this chapter. I'm sharing this to show you that there are others out there who feel your pain and to let you know that our thoughts are based on real-life experience. With that preface, here's our story…

I lived in Japan for close to six years. Five years of that time were spent teaching English full-time in two different tiny, rural towns in southern Mie Prefecture. Both of these towns were so remote that no expressways had been built to connect them with the rest of the bustling country most people think of when they think of the metropolises of Japan. The nearest movie theater was at least a two-hour drive away. Even for the people who lived in Mie Prefecture, most of them never ventured as far south as I was living. When people in the nearest big city, Nagoya, heard where I lived, they would look at me like I was a crazy mountain man. Mountains and ocean were really all that were there—and a lot of great people who had really big hearts.

During this time I met my wife, Mai, a sweet local girl whom I had to beg over several years to go on a date with me. After I finally got the chance to show her my charm on some dates, we married and started having a family right away.

While in Japan I was building up my language skills and studying to take a language proficiency exam to be given that December. This was my original pie-in-the-sky goal when I came to Japan several years prior: to pass the highest-level language proficiency exam. The teaching employment contract I had initially had expired in August of that year. Since then I had been studying at least twelve hours a day in preparation for this test.

We made a conscious family decision that I would not work, but rather study full-time until I took the test and live off our savings during this period. My wife, twenty-month-old daughter, and I moved to a cheap rental house in my wife's hometown. This house was owned by a wealthy man who also owned the sawmill located at the end of the street. It was a nice house for what we paid. One of the amenities was that every day at noon in the summertime the house was shaded by the mountain next to it when the sun moved far enough across the sky. I particularly enjoyed watching about fifteen wild monkeys that lived on the mountain and would regularly cross the street in front of us carrying the baby monkeys on their backs. My wife hated that they would toss our garbage everywhere, but being from the Midwest, I thought it was rather funny. We also had a very kind neighbor who was a retired Coast Guard officer and liked to grow flowers.

Our daughter was quite a handful, especially since my wife was pregnant. With my in-laws living close by, there was a lot of help, and everyone pitched in to give me the time I needed to study quietly at home.

Our first daughter had been born fairly healthy, but had needed to be delivered via C-section and was kept in an incubator for about a week. My recollection isn't clear, but the medical condition was basically something related to my wife's blood pressure. The hospital scheduled a C-section, and our daughter was born one week prior to the expected due date. As far as I could tell, it was nothing major, but in Japan they tend to require patients be hospitalized for rather minor conditions. This practice was more than I had ever seen in the United States.

Because of the circumstances regarding our first-born daughter, the doctors and nurses took care to watch for any signs of abnormality in Mai's second pregnancy. At every doctor's visit we left reassured that all signs were positive and we were going to have a healthy baby boy.

Mai was very active during her second pregnancy. Not only is she very active in general, but she also had our daughter to chase around. During that time she always seemed to feel great and felt the baby kicking and moving in her womb.

Having a happy wife and healthy daughter and expecting a healthy newborn on December 1st, I thought all things were looking good and that there was a lot to be happy about, even though I was unemployed and studying like crazy.

In late October, while my wife was making lunch, she told me she was a little worried because the baby hadn't moved since the night before. I blew it off because there seemed to be no end to the old wives' tales going around that small town in regard to pregnancy. I told her to give it some time, and if she still felt the same concern in a couple of hours, we could go to the hospital.

Later that night we finished dinner, and Mai said she had felt some small movements, but far fewer than normal so she was concerned. The local hospital had a hotline for expectant mothers to call if they had questions, and so she called. They asked a couple of routine questions and sounded as skeptical as I felt. They let her know that if she were really that concerned, she could come in and get checked out, but everything was probably fine. It was around 8 P.M., and Mai opted to go in and get checked out.

Mai: The hospital was reluctant to have me come in. My town was small, and they had only one OB/GYN whom the city hospital had to pay nearly double the average salary for him to move to our rural town. When the expecting mothers came in, the hospital staff didn't like to

call the doctor after hours if it wasn't for a delivery because
they knew he had to make a trip back to the hospital from
home. Since he was the only OB/GYN, they tried to let
him rest whenever they could and not call him unless they
really had to. They were not excited about me coming in.
They tried to tell me it was natural for the baby not to
move and that he was probably sleeping. I'm a worrier by
nature, so I forced the issue and told them I was coming
anyway and would be there shortly.

I took Mai and my daughter in the car to the hospital and was
relieved to see one of my friends on duty as the floor nurse.
She told me that most mothers get worried from time to time
and it was probably nothing, and that they'd check Mai out
and then have us on our way as soon as they could. I had a seat
in the waiting room with my daughter, while my wife went in
the back room to be checked out.

In traditional Japanese society, it was very common for the
men to be completely separated from anything having to do
with childbirth. While Japanese society is changing, during
the time we were there birthing babies was not treated as a
family event, but rather as something that women take care
of and then afterward bring the men in to see the baby. Two
years prior when Mai was pregnant with our daughter, when
I requested to be in the room when my daughter was born,
the hospital staff gave me a lot of strange looks. My boss at
the time thought I was an idiot for requesting the day off

to be with my wife at the hospital and rejected my request completely. I only share this to explain the cultural context of these events.

———✺———

Mai: The nurse took me into the examination room and put a device on my belly to listen to the baby's heartbeat. After about five minutes of monitoring the baby, they told me everything was all right. There was a heartbeat, and it sounded normal. The nurse smiled at me and told me that everything was going to be fine and there was nothing to worry about; I was just being an overly concerned mother. Less than a minute later she ran over and put an oxygen mask on me and told me she was calling the doctor right away.

———✺———

I was in the waiting room with our daughter when the whirlwind began. I had no idea about the ride I was in for, and it's only through God's grace and people coming to my side that I was able to make it through what would be the worst period of my life.

My friend, the nurse, came back and told me it would probably be best if I had the grandparents watch our daughter. I don't remember exactly what happened next, but I do remember meeting my in-laws in the parking lot and running with them up to the fifth floor where my wife was waiting.

I felt as if I were having an out-of-body experience because the exchange between the doctor, my in-laws, and me was so surreal. While my Japanese was sharp, it was hard for me to follow the doctor's vagueness, my father-in-law's strong local dialect, and my mother-in-law's questions, with my daughter squirming around at the same time.

What I thought I had heard was that it was going to be a choice between the life of my wife or that of my unborn son. That totally blew me away, and I was shell-shocked. I felt as if I were losing all control. My father-in-law seemed pretty passionate about one side of this argument, and my mother-in-law's opinion wasn't nearly as firm but seemed to be in agreement with that of her husband.

I don't know for how long this went on (it was probably about two or three minutes) when I finally told everyone firmly to just stop. I asked if this was a choice between my wife and the baby, and that is when everyone looked at me realizing I had not understood what was going on.

The doctor looked at the ground. My father-in-law looked as if he didn't know what to say. My mother-in-law spoke slowly and clearly and explained that there was something wrong with the baby. The baby was going to die, and they needed to do something quickly to have any chance at preventing this from happening. They didn't know exactly what was wrong, but there were two options. The first option was to put my wife in an ambulance and drive her to a major hospital about two hours away where they had all the proper medical equipment to save babies. The problem with this option was that the doctor was sure the baby would die before the ambulance arrived at the hospital. The second option was to perform a C-section immediately, pull the baby out, and do whatever they could do to save our son; but since they didn't have all the proper medical equipment at that hospital, the chance of him surviving was low and he would probably die.

What a wonderful set of options, I remember thinking to myself sarcastically while everything started to blur. I wish I had done something brave or amazing, but I didn't. I felt totally helpless and absolutely worthless. I was lost, and at that point my whole mental function starting shutting down. My father-in-law was of the opinion that it was best to pull out the baby there and let the doctor do the best with what he had at his disposal in this remote, small-town, underequipped hospital.

At that point anyone who had a suggestion about the two impossible choices was welcome to share it, and I agreed with my father-in-law. The doctor kept looking at the ground while he left quickly to start preparing for the emergency C-section.

—— ✺ ——

Mai: They transferred me to the birthing room, and the baby's heartbeat kept getting slower and slower. I started to panic and got really worried. The doctor appeared and presented my options to me: either take my child out here in this hospital or get in an ambulance to go to the next big city and hope the baby would live long enough to be treated there, but he probably wouldn't make it. He said my father and Drew thought it would be best to take my son out immediately and try to save him.

The panic and fear kept growing inside of me. They told me to stay calm, but how could I stay calm when they were telling me my son might die? I didn't understand. One week earlier the doctor had checked on my baby and me and said everything was normal. Now he was saying he had no idea why this was happening. What had changed? What did I do over the last week to make this happen?

They asked me to wait while they brought in an ultrasound machine. I kept going into a deeper and deeper panic about what was going on. If my son were going to die why didn't they hurry up and do something? Why did we need an ultrasound machine? Was there really time for that? I was frustrated because it had taken so long for the doctor to get to the hospital to begin with and even longer for them to get an ultrasound machine into the room.

All of a sudden every face in the room froze. The doctor and nurse looked at one another for a moment, and then he turned toward me with his eyes on the floor. He told me my son's heart had stopped and he was sorry.

When I went to the hospital, I was so relieved because I heard my son's heart beating. Why did he die now? He was just alive; I just heard his heartbeat and he was fine! I couldn't believe he actually died. It wasn't coming into my heart. I believed that he was still alive; I was sure of it because I had just heard his heartbeat a few moments ago.

I blamed myself. I thought I could have saved my son had I gone to the hospital earlier. I blamed myself for moving around as much as I did. I believed I didn't do as much as I could to protect him. I felt awful, having failed as a mother to fulfill the most important duty of all: to protect my baby's life.

I started to panic even more. I didn't cry because I was losing my mind. The nurse came and grabbed my hand very tightly and told me it was good to cry. She told me it's better to cry. I started balling my eyes out and lost control. They asked if I wanted to see my husband, and I said yes.

I remember seeing the hospital staff tearing up and being noticeably disturbed. The doctor came out and couldn't look at any of us. My friend, the nurse, was crying with tears streaming down her face, but she did her best to remain composed since Japanese culture strongly frowns upon showing any emotion. I could feel the tension in the air, and behind the open doorI could see the other nurses with their heads down and wiping their eyes. The doctor stared at the floor and mumbled something to the effect that he had done what he could, but my son was no longer alive.

At that time I wasn't sure if I was in shock; I felt very weak and helpless. The situation at the hospital had been so far out of my control since we arrived that I was just barely hanging on. I became robotic, and even the feelings of weakness and helplessness that I had faded and I was just numb. Looking back, I was certainly in shock. The staff told me they needed to remove our son from my wife's body, but she was hysterical and needed me to come and calm her down so they could perform the C-section.

After I was taken into the back room, the first wave of the true gravity of the situation hit me. Mai was in a hospital bed prepped for surgery, with a black line drawn on her stomach for where the incision would be made, and she was shaking her head violently from left to right and talking like a baby.

Seconds seemed like hours. I stood there and watched her for couple of moments to try to take it all in. I had no idea what to do. The nurse walked over to Mai and told her I was in the room and that they were going to leave, and the two nurses got up and walked out quickly. With my wife flailing, I went over to her and sat down on a stool next to her bed.

Sitting next to her and stroking her forehead, I tried to calm her down, but what she was saying was incredible. While I am a strong believer in God, I am not a believer in supernatural, out-of-body experiences; however, this is what we experienced.

Mai had lost complete control of herself, and my dead son was being channeled through her. He was saying things that sounded like baby talk, "Ba-ba-boo, Ba-ba-boo" and "I wanted to play with Grandpa. I wanted to see Grandma!" He said other things as well, and it was all mixed in with the "Ba-ba-boo, Ba-ba-boo." It was very, very painful and sad to hear.

I had never seen anyone in this condition before, and I knew Mai well enough to be able to tell this was not her speaking. I just kept stroking and kissing her forehead and trying to get her to calm down. If I could do it all over again, I would hold her and shut my mouth and listen more rather than interrupt what was probably the only time in my life I would ever witness anything like this. After what felt like a long time later, Mai seemed to return to being as close to normal as anyone could hope for, and they took her to the operating room to remove our dead son.

—————❧—————

Mai: This was an experience I would not have believed if it had not happened to me. I had no control of my body and believe that my dead son was talking through me. He kept saying, "I wanted to be born! Ba-ba-boo! I wanted to meet Grandma! I wanted to be born, I really wanted to be born!"

I was conscious but had no control of what was coming out of my mouth. Drew asked if I wanted him to get my mother, but I couldn't respond. I could hear him ask the nurse to have my mother come back, and when she came in I could hear her, but I couldn't open my eyes. My head kept shaking back and forth violently, and our son kept talking to us. He kept repeating over and over how he wanted to be born, how he wanted to play, and how he wanted to meet his grandma and grandpa.

After some time, my son stopped talking. I was sobbing and not myself. My mother told me to take care and hold on tight during the surgery before she and Drew left the room.

My mother lost her first child when he was only a couple of months old, and I felt horrible because I knew this was hurting her too. I felt so awful putting her through this pain. Everything about the situation felt horrible.

I was conscious and kept thrashing my head back and forth during the surgery, but it wasn't me. I felt that it was my son shaking his head back and forth and how terrible this was. The violent shaking of my head was so bad that the nurses had to hold my head as tightly as they could so that I wouldn't shake myself off the table while the doctor removed my dead son.

Later, I wondered why I kept shaking my head during the C-section. I think it's because our daughter was a C-section, and in Japan they tell us you can have up to three C-sections. This was the second one, limiting us to having only one more child. I believe it was my son telling me that he didn't want to come out of a C-section, but rather be an induced labor birth so I could still have more children. (Note: While Japanese doctors insist there is a three-cut limit, our American doctors have since informed us that is not true.)

Now it was late, and somewhere along the way my sister-in-law had taken my daughter. My parents-in-law and I waited in the basement hallway of the hospital until the C-section was completed. Awkward silence is a complete understatement about what we were feeling. None of us knew what to think or do. I tried to sit down but couldn't. I tried to stand, but it didn't feel right. It was that odd transitional time between when something really big happens and when the full impact of it hits you. I had a lot of questions, but most of them were about what to do next. After what seemed like forever, the hospital staff came out and let us know the surgery was completed.

The staff brought us into a private room, and then they brought in my child. I can't fully describe what it's like to hold your own dead son. He was full-term, so he looked like and was around the same size as every other newborn I had ever seen. When I saw him in my arms, it looked as if he would just wake up and everything would be all right. He looked the same as my daughter did when she was born. My in-laws and I took turns holding him until the nurses wheeled my wife into the room. The nurses put my son next to Mai in the bed so she could see him and hold him while recovering.

Maybe it's just me or maybe it's a cultural attitude toward death, but I wasn't big on doing much besides holding the baby. My wife and mother-in-law really wanted to check him out. They were peeking at his eye color, the shapes of his toes and fingers, and all that. To each their own, but that was not something I was comfortable with.

Mai: The nurse asked me if I'd like to have our son in the room. I told her yes. I wanted to have the chance to make a memory with my baby. He died, so other people might not have been open to holding him but it was going to be my first and last time to see him, so I wanted to make sure he was in my memory. He's my son, and even though I felt a lot of physical pain having just had a C-section, I had to hold him just like I held my daughter after she was born because he was mine and I loved him. I still love him. I knew there was only going to be one chance to see him, so I looked at him, felt him, and made a solid memory of him in my mind. I checked out the size of his hands, the shape of his feet, and felt his head and his hair; I did everything I could to make sure I never forgot him.

In Japan, we usually leave the dead out in people's homes for one night, and usually the bodies have a straight mouth and look peaceful at best. My son was left in our room for the night, and the next morning when I looked over at him I couldn't believe it, he had a smile on his face! Of all the dead people I've seen, I have never seen a smiling face on any of them. The head nurse came in that morning and said the same thing to me. I am convinced it was his way of telling me that he was happy to be able to spend just a little bit of time with me. I am so sorry that our time together was so short.

I didn't feel any fear of death or feel creepy about a dead body. He was my son, and I loved him so much. My little baby was going to have the chance for me to hold him in my arms. He did have his father's face, I remember that, and it was amazing how much he looked like his dad.

The next couple of days in the hospital were awkward and uncomfortable. The staff put us in a private room on another floor away from the maternity ward so we wouldn't hear babies crying, and they kept the traffic in our room and the general area as minimal as possible. They showed us a lot of compassion and provided anything we needed right away. One thing they did that I didn't know what to think about at the time was to put a lot of dry ice packs under our son and let us keep him in the room for a couple of days. I'm squeamish when it comes to death, but everyone else thought this was great. When Mai's close family came to visit, they all thought being able to see our son was a good thing. Quite frankly I didn't know what to think, but I wasn't about to do anything to upset my wife during all this and let it be. I loved him, and part of me wanted to hold him and build memories with him as my wife was doing. I wanted to apologize to him. I wanted to pray for him; I wanted to pray with him. I wanted to hold him and bring him back to life somehow. Other times I just wanted to be on the other side of the room because he was a corpse. There were a few times when I wished they would take him out of the room so I wouldn't have to look at him anymore. Several times I just wanted to crawl under my wife's hospital bed and cry.

Mai: I remember being so sad and wishing I would die. They put us on the geriatric floor so we wouldn't hear all the babies crying to upset us more. Hearing the old people on the floor get grumpy with one another and clearing their throats all the time was amusing to me for some reason and helped me feel a little bit better. I kept the door slightly open so I could hear the bickering between the grumpy men and the nurses, and also so the nurses could come in and out easily. Every time they had to come in for anything and knock first, I could tell it was a strange and uncomfortable situation for them, so I just left the door cracked open to help them.

A nurse came in and informed me that the nurse's station knew to turn away any visitors and not to tell anyone what room I was in. That was a huge help. They even made sure to take my name off the door (common practice in Japan), so if anyone came looking for me they wouldn't be able to find me.

All of my sisters visited. All of us talked about how we had been so excited to have a boy born in the family. My mother's child whom she lost was a boy, and I am one of three sisters. Everyone in my family was looking forward to the first boy in our family, so everyone came in and checked out his little hands, feet, and face to see what he looked like.

The hospital staff were kind. For the very last time I would ever see him, they dressed my son in some baby clothes and put him in a little baby holding box, with some flowers and some baby toys too. That was the last time I would see my son on this earth. After that last time, my mother and father took him to their house. In Japan we leave the dead out for one night in the home, and to keep that custom my parents took him and left.

Then it hit me that this was really the end. It was both the beginning and the end of my time with him. I knew there was nothing I could do. Because of the C-section I couldn't walk, let alone leave the hospital, so I couldn't spend the one day he had left with us at my parents' house. I was so sad. I was his mother, and I wanted to be with him every second he was here with us. I couldn't even do that for him, and so I felt guilty for a long time.

Something I remember often is that from our window at the hospital we could see one of the largest buildings in town, which a successful business mogul acquaintance of mine had recently purchased. He had painted it purple and put his company's logo on the top of it for the entire city to see. I remember thinking about how many people from the hospital look at that and have far more important things to worry about aside from purple buildings and empire building. It struck me that all the wealth in the world could not bring my son back. Modern medicine, or at least as close to modern medicine as that hospital had, couldn't save him. I wondered how many dying people had stared out of this hospital's windows at this same building and had the same thoughts I was having.

The mental twists and mind games began right away: Why me? Why us? Why did this happen? Why an innocent baby? Why not me? Was this God's way of punishing me for something I did? My son didn't do anything wrong. I've done more than enough in my life to deserve this more than that helpless innocent baby ever possibly could have done. The questions kept coming faster and faster with no good answers. With my mind racing, I can assure you my thoughts were not easy or rational. It's not as if I just handed this tragedy over to God and walked away smiling that it was God's will and I would be a faithful servant. There were a lot of unanswered questions and a lot of tears. We were in real, raw pain and felt absolutely hopeless. This was a very difficult test of faith.

The conclusion I kept coming back to was that this is what God wanted. We didn't know why, how, or for what purpose, but this was what He wanted. While it hurt so badly, we had to trust in Him and have faith that it was for His purpose.

Mai: *I stayed in the hospital room with the window curtains wide open and looked out at the sky. My heart was destroyed. I was sad and depressed and felt I had no reason to live. I looked out the window every day. The sky was a perfect blue and sunny. I felt as if the heavens had opened up to show me my son had made it there. I felt the skies were there to show me that heaven really is there, and to remind me that my son had a smiling face. These things were there to remind me that there is hope and to lift my spirits. God was telling me that my child died, but holding out hope is right. By looking out at that beautiful sky so much during my hospital stay, I felt God was talking to me.*

My heart had sunk so low, and yet for some reason I felt as though someone had wrapped their arms around me and was holding my heart in a huge bundle and protecting me from anything more. I was in a sterile, clinical, and cold hospital room, yet I felt I was wrapped in this warm embrace of kindness in my wrecked state. Later I was sure this was God holding me in his arms and protecting me from any more harm while I was in this low point in my life.

I kept wondering what my son was doing in heaven. I wondered if he were smiling. I wondered if he could talk. I wondered if he knew how much his mother loved him.

This was when Drew asked if I wanted to name him. In Japan, stillborn babies are not given names on their death certificates, but I wanted to name him Reagan. Drew cracked a smile and agreed. He told me that was the name of a very popular American president from the past. I don't know anything about American politics, so it was totally by chance, but I knew our son had to have a name.

My older sister worked at the hospital, so she stopped in often to see how I was doing. She wasn't comfortable touching the baby, but she helped me by coming in and sharing some funny stories with me about some of the other patients. She knew I was having a really hard time and still came in and shared stories that made my C-section incision hurt from laughing so much. It was much needed relief and helped me feel better even if it was just for a couple of moments at a time.

I was grateful for my sisters and parents, but at this time I really wanted Drew next to me. As special as my friends are and as much as I appreciate them, I just wasn't up to seeing them. I felt very comfortable around my husband and parents and slightly less so around my sisters, but I really wanted to be left alone with Drew.

Later the nurses asked me if I took a picture of my son. I said no, and they told me everyone takes a picture. I guess it's just the way I am that I thought I shouldn't. Looking back, it probably would have been better to have had at least one photo to show his brothers and sisters in the future to help share Reagan's memory.

Several different nurses on different shifts came in and reassured me that what happened was not because of something I did, and I shouldn't feel responsible. They shared some encouraging words with me and said it probably happened for some reason we can't understand and to do my best to keep pressing on and living well. Their words were kind, but I still had a deep sense of guilt about being the mother of a dead baby.

I had recently made a total ass of myself to the local pastor. This isn't the place to go into detail, but I had some serious egg on my face and I had to go hat-in-hand to ask for help. The grace that the pastor showed me was astounding, and he dropped everything to come and help.

My father-in-law is a carpenter, and the day that I called the pastor my father-in-law had made a coffin for Reagan. I didn't know he did this at the time, but they didn't have coffins small enough for Reagan so he made one. Looking back on it now, I think about what a very tough, loving thing it was to do. I know I couldn't have done that in the mindset I was in, and I will always be thankful for the times my father-in-law stepped in to help.

Mai: This was very hard on my parents too. This was their second time dealing with a death of a baby boy. The first was my mother's firstborn, who was only a couple of months old. After she had him they had three girls, so we always felt God wasn't going to let anyone in our family have boys. In our town in Japan, it is still very warm in October. My mom told me that when she took Reagan home, she put the air conditioning on high so his body still looked fine. She said he looked as if he were sleeping.

I'm assuming most of you reading this are not familiar with Japanese death customs, but basically they keep the body in the home overnight on the day before the cremation. They also put out things that the deceased liked, such as food, cigarettes, beer, and so…My in-laws pulled out all the stops and gathered all the snacks and treats my child could have ever wanted to lay out next to his body.

That night the pastor and his wife came to my in-law's house to do a little service they had prepared. My wife's parents followed along as best they could. They come from a Buddhist background, so participating in a Christian service and singing hymns such as "What a Friend We Have in Jesus" after losing Reagan must have seemed very odd.

After the mini-service we sat down and talked for a little while. During that time I remember my daughter kept trying to get into the baby snacks laid out for Reagan, and she inadvertently flipped over the little coffin he was in a couple of times. Traditional Japanese homes do not have chairs; they sit on the floor and have low tables, so for Reagan to be laid out in a coffin on the floor was normal. My daughter didn't know any better, bless her heart, but it was such a mental trip to watch someone so innocent do something that awful and have no idea what was going on. Once again I found myself lost between caring for and loving my son and being spooked about a corpse. I don't know why I found it funny that our daughter was eating all the snacks laid out for our son. The spread of children's treats and snacks laid out for Reagan included all the things my daughter and every other kid loved; there's no way she could have resisted. If there was anything that gave everyone a little break from the grief and guilt we all felt, it was the occasional dark humor that we experienced.

———— ∞∞ ————

Mai: *Due to the C-section I couldn't walk, and I had to stay in the hospital. I felt horrible not being able to attend my own child's funeral. I kept thinking about how I wanted to be there, feeling guilty about not being able to be there, and playing the mental movie of what was going on. I felt I was a horrible mother for not being there with Reagan.*

Looking back, I think it was more meaningful for me to have the chance to hold my son and sleep with him in my hospital bed than to actually attend the funeral. Of course, I wish I had been able to do both, but having held Reagan in my arms in my hospital bed is something that means a lot to me to this day.

My middle sister would often stay with me in my hospital room when Drew and my parents had to leave to take care of things. She was taking care of the house most of the time while my parents were helping us. I don't remember what she said when she visited, but it all turned into noise because it was just a bunch of stuff about the house and the little disagreements at home that didn't interest me. What she said didn't matter; what mattered was that she was there.

———— ∞∞ ————

I spent every night on a cot in the hospital with Mai, and fatigue started to take over. I don't remember whether I got any rest for the following day. The night of the small service we held for our son was sad, but the next day was to be another one of the toughest days of my life.

Mai: For two or three nights I couldn't sleep. I was wide-awake and too scared to close my eyes. I was thinking so much and wondering why this happened. The nurse gave me a sleeping pill, and I kept asking Drew if it was a good idea to take it. Finally, after he tired of me asking him over and over about the pill, he ordered me to take it. I finally got some sleep.

I ended up taking sleeping pills to help me get to sleep for about a month. Every day I was so afraid to close my eyes and was terrified of what I would see or think if I did. I'm not sure if I was scared to accept that Reagan really died, or if I was scared that I might see images of the most terrifying moments leading up to him dying, but it was just too scary to close my eyes.

Every night I took one of those pills and held my husband's hand until I passed out. He stayed up with me, and on some nights he fell asleep first, but he held my hand until I fell asleep every single night.

The law mandates cremation for all corpses in Japan. I'm not an expert, but I believe that this is because of a lack of land and historical concerns about spreading infection. If my memory is correct, full-term unborn babies fall into a gray area under the law, but at the time it made sense to follow tradition and have Reagan's body cremated.

The morning after Reagan had spent the night in the home of my in-laws, I drove to their house from the hospital. I went upstairs to put on a suit to deliver him to the cremation parlor. I was having a hard time keeping it together. I put on a black suit I had purchased to attend a funeral for the wife of the superintendent of schools a few years ago. It was one of the most moving funerals I had ever attended. About three hundred people were there. Each of the couple's three adult children stood up and spoke to a large photograph of their mother about the memories they had and how much they loved her. I was remembering how Mai and I had attended this funeral on our first anniversary after we had been fighting for a couple of days. Walking out of that service we held each other tightly and vowed we would work hard to have as much love in our house as that family had. I remember putting my black suit away that day and hoping I wouldn't need it again for a very long time. I certainly never imagined the next time I'd wear it would be for the death of one of my own children.

After getting dressed, I took some deep breaths before walking downstairs. I loved my son, I really did. But I couldn't help thinking about how long he had been dead and wondering how long you could keep a dead body out like this without it starting to smell or decompose. I told myself that if there was anyone who was going to carry him in this form to his final resting place, it had to be his dad. I owed him that after how horrible a father I had been to him so far. I knew he deserved so much better than me. I felt guilty about not being as open to checking out his dead body like everyone else. I felt guilty for not wanting to have his corpse around as much as everyone else. I was disappointed in myself for not being able to save him. I blamed myself for not being good enough to be his dad.

When I got downstairs, Reagan's coffin was sitting near the front door for me. The lid of the coffin was closed, covering him. I was secretly very thankful for that. I didn't want to see any more; I wasn't strong enough for that. I picked him up in his little coffin and sat down in the back seat of the car where my in-laws were waiting. As I held Reagan in my lap, I started to feel overwhelmed. I'm a very strong person who almost never cries, but I felt it coming. I took some deep breaths. It seemed as if every moment we were in the car was passing so slowly. The pressure on everyone of not knowing what to say and trying to hold back emotion, and the pain of having my baby Reagan, who was too young to die and too small even to find a coffin for, riding in my lap on the way to deliver him to be incinerated to ashes was just too much. It was a miracle I didn't have a total meltdown in the car. I kept telling myself over and over again, "Not now, not now, breathe, breathe." Every time I felt Reagan move when we hit a bump in the road or turned, it kept pushing me to my limits, and I was reaching my breaking point.

When we arrived at the crematorium, the undertaker came out to meet us and bowed very solemnly. He guided us silently to a large room in the back of the building where I had to place my son on a stone slab that moves the bodies into the kiln. They had made a special mark for me as a guide for where to put the coffin on the stone slab because the coffin was smaller than that of any of their usual customers. Looking down at the slab, with its black burned color, the rollers that moved it back and forth, and then to the blackness of the depths of the place where they were going to burn my son's body made me feel as if I were in a horror movie. His coffin was so much smaller than the slab was designed for; it was too much for me to take in.

Leaving him there was such a hard thing to do. I had been growing more and more concerned about how long he had been dead and out in the open air, but this was it. This was really it. It took everything in me to lay him down where they had marked. I tried to be gentle when I laid him down, and I don't know why. I knew what they were about to do to his body. I looked at the coffin on the slab, and looked again at where it would slide his tiny little body to be burned, and then my imagination started to kick in with visuals of what it would look like while he burned. I knew I had to leave before I became a total wreck. Turning to walk out of there made me feel as if I were abandoning Reagan and burning him like rubbish. I walked out with my head down, and during the entire ride home I cried while everyone else in the car was silent.

When we got back to my in-laws' house, I went directly upstairs and completely broke down. How was this fair? Why would God allow such gruesome things as burning babies to be a part of this world? How could I ever consider myself a man after not wanting to be around my son's body during his entire time with us? I didn't want to see his body anymore and was getting what I wanted, so why was I upset now?

All of these emotions were overpowering. Being that vulnerable, even with some of the best people in the world surrounding me and helping me, I felt no one in the world could understand what I was going through. I don't know how long I was up there. When I stopped crying, I stared at the walls until I felt I could keep it together. Eventually I was able to change out of my suit and head back downstairs. All of my in-laws heard me crying upstairs and didn't know what to say or do. All of us pretended to ignore each other until it was time to get the ashes.

I don't remember now how long the cremation took, but with cremations in Japan they pick out one of the bones from the neck after cremation to keep with the ashes. Traditionally the father does this, and then the ashes are given to the parents or next of kin for burial. I was not up to this. There was no way I was going to pick through Reagan's ashes for bones for tradition's sake. I asked my father-in-law if he would do it, and he agreed. I think if he had not been there to do that for me and I had been forced to do it, I would have lost my sanity. I believe the textbook definition for this is *culture shock,* but that term does not even come close to describing how far

34

down the path I had found myself.

My father-in-law took care of a lot more than that. He also made plot arrangements in the graveyard for us. The point of this book is not to delve into burial traditions in Japan, but long story short, in the back of my mind I had begun to worry if we'd be able to handle the expenses associated with these end-of-life services. I hated myself for thinking about money at a time like this, but I couldn't help it. A few months before, I had read an exposé article about the so-called "death industry" in Japan. The article claimed Japanese funerals cost nearly as much as weddings because many less-than-reputable undertakers had gotten into the business, and they knew that families wouldn't argue about the price at the time of a loss of a loved one, so they were charging astronomical prices. One of the significant expenses cited was the plot where the loved one would be interned. I knew with our financial situation there was no way I'd be able to afford any land in Japan, even if it was just a plot in the graveyard. My father-in-law must have known that too, so he arranged for our son to be interned in his plot, gave half of his plot to us to use when our gravestone was ready, and also got us a great deal with the gravestone maker, who was one of his drinking buddies. This was amazing because there is no way we could have done any of this without my father-in-law's help. We just didn't have the money for it, and once again he saved the day.

Picking out a gravestone was difficult. I was unemployed, and we had budgeted just enough for me to study for the test I mentioned earlier and then to get a job immediately. We never imagined we'd need to buy a gravestone, so it was quite a balancing act to get what we felt was respectable and also within our budget. The gravestone makers, as I mentioned, were friends with my father-in-law so we did get an incredible deal. They etched an English Bible passage for us into the stone. It was Matthew 5:14, "You are the light of the world." Those guys were very friendly and kind to us. They had been drinking pals of my father-in-law for decades and shared many funny stories of their late-night adventures with him to keep the mood as light as possible. They were very careful and kept asking me to check on the etching every step of the way because they had never etched anything in English before.

When all the preparations were done, the actual burial just felt so wrong. I don't know if this is traditional in Japan or not, but initially we put our son's remains in my father-in-law's plot to be moved later once our gravestone was finished. In all the Western funerals I have been to, I've just shown up at the gravesite and there has been a hole in the ground. No such luck in our case. My father-in-law pulled out a shovel from his pickup truck, and it felt gruesome to be there. We started to dig a hole to put Reagan's urn in. The feelings of shame, guilt, and sadness on top of how sick and twisted it felt to be digging my own baby's grave were too much. Once again I felt myself on the emotional edge just trying to hold it all together.

Something happened, and I really wish I could remember what took place. I don't have any clue what it was now that it's been so long, and I'm kicking myself. Somehow God showed us mercy, and something really funny happened right then that made everyone laugh. It was something pretty comical because even those of us who were tearing up couldn't stop laughing. My father-in-law did something by accident while digging, and it was absolutely hilarious. Thank God that happened because it helped all of us pull through without falling to pieces.

That was the last day of having more and more unthinkable tasks piled on me. I remember several times that week lying on my cot in the hospital and praying to God that He would not force me to have to experience these things ever again: a dead baby, a cremation, an internment, a wife who needed more from me than I knew how to give, and all the other things in between. I don't remember ever being as bombarded with so many of the most impossible things to do in my life at one time. I prayed for this to please never happen to me again.

When Mai was discharged, we returned from the hospital to my in-law's home; it was not easy. The plan was that we would stay there so they could help nurse Mai back to health while she was recovering from surgery and provide emotional support too.

———⬖⬖⬖———

Mai: At first we went back to my mom's house. My mom had done so much for us, but after staying there for a night, I could tell it wasn't going to work. They were my family and I loved them, but it was tough to be around my daughter. For some reason her voice triggered my feelings of guilt, and I couldn't take it. She wanted me to hold her and play with her, but I couldn't because of the surgery. Being around my family was hard too. I just wasn't myself and needed some time on my own with Drew.

I asked my mom if she could take our daughter while I healed, both physically and mentally. Thankfully she agreed. My mother took our daughter back and forth to daycare, put her to bed at night, played with her, everything. I don't know what I would have done without all that help.

Coming home without Reagan was one of the hardest realities I've ever experienced. I felt as though it was all my fault. I looked back and blamed myself for not going to the hospital earlier. I blamed myself for moving around as much as I did while carrying him. I blamed myself for not taking care of my baby and letting him die.

All I could do is cry. I cried and cried and cried. I didn't understand why Reagan had to die. I didn't know whom else to blame but me. I felt as if someone had grabbed me

*and thrown me farther down than I had ever been before
and that I would never have a chance at feeling normal,
or even just bad, ever again. I hated myself. I was sure it
was better to die than to have to deal with this pain. I had
fallen off the edge.*

———— ◆◇◆ ————

My in-laws were fantastic in supporting us. Being attentive and caring, they took care of our daughter, delivered food several times a day, took care of our laundry, and attended to anything else we needed. That took a huge burden from us, and we were very thankful for that. If they had not been by our side and wrapped us in their love, we would never have made it.

For at least a month we took no phone calls and had no contact with the outside world. We just let Mai's family love us by taking care of the things that needed to be taken care of. I am not a model husband by any stretch, but I did the best I could to console my wife emotionally and help her heal physically from the C-section.

There were many days where we just lay around the house in mourning. Sometimes we felt we failed in our only reason for living. Other days we felt as if our souls had been ripped from our bodies. In all of my life's failures, disappointments, and downswings, I have never felt as if I hit rock bottom as hard or have descended so low as I did then.

We had a lot of quiet time, and I really struggled in my

faith. I kept asking God, Why? What did I do? What is this punishment for? What did Reagan do to deserve this? Our agony seemed to linger and make us feel as if we were rotting from the inside out.

A couple of weeks later I started to get e-mails from friends in the United States asking how Mai was coming along and if we had scheduled a date for the C-section yet. They did not know we had lost Reagan. At first I ignored them, but after more e-mails started rolling in I knew it would probably be best to say something.

I decided to write a mass e-mail. I don't remember exactly what it said, but it was short and to the point. Effectively it let everyone know that the baby had died, my wife and I felt horrible, and we probably wouldn't be in contact with anyone and would like to be left alone for a while. Everyone understood, and the few responses I did receive consisted of short words of comfort. It was a relief not to get any e-mails asking questions I didn't want to answer. We were able to continue our time of healing in peace, or so I thought.

Mai: Drew dealt with this by spending a lot of time on the computer. Most of the time I had nothing to say and neither did he. I lay in bed with him sitting next to me passing time on the Internet. Many days we barely spoke.

Around three weeks later, Drew wanted to go for a little walk. I was supposed to be moving around while healing, plus we were getting cabin fever, so we decided to walk outside at night when no one would see us. We walked slowly up the narrow street behind our house a little way. That road went up the mountainside and led to a bird's-eye view of our house, but my body wasn't ready for that. We walked about fifty feet up and back down. It felt liberating to get out of the house even for a couple of minutes.

After a few weeks, Drew would go shopping at night for little things we wanted or needed. We weren't up to seeing people, so he would pull his hat down real low to try to hide his face, but since he was the only white person in town it didn't do much good. It was actually kind of funny to see him try to hide.

Drew likes to run. I didn't want to be alone and we didn't want to see anyone, so he would take me to a remote mountain logging road where he could run up and down a straight stretch of the road in private. I would sit in a folding chair he had packed in the trunk for me and watch without him leaving my sight while he exercised. I was still so scared to be alone and needed to feel him near me. I don't think he always understood why I needed this and I don't either. I just really needed him close to me during those really hard times.

Exercise helped Drew start to feel better. While he was running, I used to look at the sky and wish with all my heart that God would give Reagan back to us. Why did Reagan die? Why did God do this to us? Why did He make us feel this horrible? These and many other questions were always on my mind. For some reason, when I saw Drew running and moving, I felt there was a way we could move forward. It was so difficult and yet my husband was still trying and moving; this helped me feel as though there could still be some reason to live. I wasn't sure how or why, but watching him run provided the inspiration I needed.

Drew spent a lot of time on his computer next to me while I was in bed. One day he found a beautiful photograph that he really liked. He said that he wanted to be able to take pictures like that. He looked for a camera online to learn photography with, and said that he wanted to become a photographer. We didn't know it at the time, but eventually that was to become something he was very passionate about. Drew was healing and I could tell. He provided me with hope that we might pull through this.

After a month of solitude passed, my wife was close to recovering from the C-section and the cuteness of our young and energetic daughter was wearing on our in-laws, so we began to try to move on to life as usual. I stress "began to try" because we were nowhere near ready, but we came to realize we would never be ready and it was probably best to jump back in with both feet and see what happened.

One question that everyone seemed to ask us that I didn't anticipate, but probably should have, was, "Where's your baby?" We got smacked with that one for the first time when we went to the post-birth follow-up appointment that all mothers go to. In that small town everyone recognizes one another. We went for the checkup, and sure enough many other mothers who had been expecting and recently delivered were there. All of them were talking excitedly about their newborn babies, the joys of motherhood, and everything in between relating to babies. Suddenly one of my wife's well-meaning acquaintances came over and asked with a huge smile, "Where's your baby?"

I felt as if everything stopped. I was lost for words. I froze for a moment and then looked at Mai. Words were still escaping me. My wife smiled back at the woman and kindly let her know what had happened. That poor girl went from being ecstatic to being one of the most uncomfortable people I'd ever seen. She found some reason to move away from us, and I don't blame her. I took Mai by the arm, and we sat in the waiting room down the hall so we wouldn't have to go through that again.

Episodes like that were going to be our reality for the upcoming year until everyone learned that Reagan had died. There's no avoiding this when you've gone full-term through a pregnancy. We paid the heavy emotional toll of losing Reagan and rolled with the endless painful reminders that came after.

Mai: I hated that question. I didn't want to talk about it. Everyone immediately felt very uncomfortable whenever we were asked. My close friends and family knew what had happened and didn't bring up the topic, but all of our acquaintances were in the dark. Even though I lived in a small town where everyone knew each other's business, the one piece of news I wished had been shared discreetly so we wouldn't have to answer these questions was not. There was no good way to share that we lost our baby. People didn't know how to react and neither did I. We always seemed to be asked this as soon as we started to have a guilt-free day. I wished everyone would stop asking me that question every time I heard it.

Many awkward moments were still ahead of us, and there were still a lot of tears to be shed. They say "life happens" and I guess it does, but it felt as if we had dived headfirst onto the sidewalk from a skyscraper and were just beginning to peel ourselves off. We were emotionally devastated and prayed to God to guide us because we needed help.

—∞∞∞—

Mai: I wasn't back to myself. It took about three months before I had an almost normal day. However, after about one month I was able to go shopping late at night when almost no one else was there. Having our daughter come back to us after only one month was very hard. My heart wasn't healed and I wasn't ready. When she came back, I stopped taking the sleeping pills and tried to sleep on my own. I knew it was going to be hard, but I had to try. She came back, and I did my best to keep going. I had to keep going for her. I had to keep going for Drew. The toughest thing for me was not knowing why Reagan had died.

—∞∞∞—

After our daughter came back to us, I tried to resume studying for the Japanese test I was supposed to take. Even though there was no possible way I'd be able to pass after not studying during all of this time, I didn't know what else to do.

It was tough just to press on, but I really didn't have a plan B. I felt the need to continue on the track where we had been headed—and what I had spent the last six-plus years preparing for—because that was as close to "normal" as I was going to get at that time. It was familiar and probably provided me with a sense of stability if I had realized it.

I took the highest-level Japanese language test in December of that year. It was so important to me for so long before any of this happened. This was supposed to be the pinnacle of years of hard language study, the envy of all other Japanese learners out there. This was the vaunted test that anyone who ever studies Japanese knows about. I would be able to go back to all my past Japanese instructors and show them how far I had come. Years and years of countless hours of investment in my studies were to be vindicated on this day in a test given only once a year, and my ability to prepare for it as I had this time around was never to come again. Because of the importance of this test and all of its future implications, we had spent our life savings to have the time for me to prepare. My wife believed in me enough to risk everything we had. My in-laws believed in me enough to help watch our daughter every single day while I studied.

All of the upside of passing the exam didn't seem significant anymore. All the career implications, future opportunities, business possibilities, it all seemed so petty. Who cared whether I could advance professionally by leaps and bounds if Reagan could not live? At this point all I cared about was not letting down my wife and in-laws. They had all worked so hard to support me, and I knew I'd lost all chance of passing the exam with the loss of the time I had spent grieving and taking care of Mai.

The test site was at a university far from our home, so I had to travel there the night before and stay in what's called a Business Hotel. Staying in a Business Hotel is like renting a tiny room in a dorm. My room stank of smoke from a previous patron who had probably smoked at least a pack of cigarettes in that small space the night before. I could even smell it on my pillow. There was a tiny TV that I tried to watch for an hour or so to pass the time. I was still restless, so I tried to walk up and down Main Street a few times to lift my spirits, but it did nothing except make me think about how futile so much in life is.

As I walked around, I glanced at the decorated windows on Main Street as I passed by. I saw the fancy clothes in the windows of the trendy clothing boutiques. An electronics store proudly displayed the latest and greatest of computers and cell phones. A high-class restaurant had a valet in front and a chalk sign posted near the entrance stating that they were serving some of the finest lobster. I asked myself again and again, is this what I was after? Was the point to study so hard for more stuff, better stuff? I would trade anything in the world to have Reagan back again.

Simply going through the motions of things I had planned a long time ago felt empty. I remember thinking to myself that if I actually had been studying as much as I had planned on for this test and if I had thought I had a chance of passing it, I'd probably be at least a little nervous. Instead, I was in a hotel room that stank to take a test I was going to fail because it had been what I wanted to do a long time ago.

The next day, as I approached the university where the exam was being held, I saw a bunch of nervous but hopeful test takers outside. They were smoking and double-checking their pencils to make sure they were ready for the exam. I wished my life could be so simple again. I wished Reagan were alive.

I wished I could be hopeful yet nervous about this definitive language exam. I wished I had a brand-new baby at home. Like the night before, that entire day turned into a dreary reminder of how my life was supposed to have been.

As I sat in the examination room, I could feel the tension rise when each section of the exam was handed out, and again when the time was called to an end. I overheard people asking each other what they thought the answers were, or how they thought they did. I avoided all of it and went for a walk away from the test site between sections because I couldn't fake it with others. It would be too obvious that there were gaps in my knowledge and that I was unprepared compared to others. I didn't want to risk taking away from their experience by creating awkward moments. I just wanted to witness the scenes of that day as they passed by. I didn't want to engage with anyone around me; I wanted to be left alone to watch.

Between each section of the test, I would go for the same walk away from everyone else as soon as the test monitors collected the exam papers. I'd look at my cell phone intently as if I had an important message, while making my way through the swarm of people looking for anyone with whom to discuss the exam questions. I kept staring at my phone intently until I was well out of range for anyone to strike up a conversation with me. This was the pattern I followed to break free from the crowd. I'm not sure why, but those times alone were the small respites I needed.

When the final section of the test was finished, I avoided

everyone and walked the opposite way to the train station. I was supposed to take the shuttle bus back to the station and had even already paid the fare. Being on a bus packed with people happy and excited to be done with one of the most challenging exams of their lives was not something I was in the mood for. I did about an hour loop walk away from the university and returned to find that everyone had left. The emptiness of the school, in contrast to how pregnant it had been with excited and anxious people just a short time before, stood out to me as a reflection of my life, filled with excitement and now empty. The difference was that all those people got to go home alive.

There was no way I could sit next to someone on a bus and make small talk with all these thoughts going through my head. Rather than ride on a city bus, I kept walking toward the station. It was cold, the streets were empty, the town felt lonely, it was getting darker and darker, and I just wanted to get to my destination; once again, the parallels of my trudging through a cold, empty, and dark life jumped out at me as I walked to the station.

Thankfully I was the only foreigner going south on the train. All of the other foreigners at the station were test takers, and if they had seen me they certainly would have struck up a conversation. The test location was far north for me, but for everyone else coming from the more populated areas of the region, this site was considered the deep south and unfairly remote for them to have to travel to. I remembered plenty of times during my years in Japan wishing that I lived in one of the bigger cities. I remembered wanting to be able to hop on one of the rail lines that would take me to the swank areas, the nightclubs. I had often thought of the fun I was missing out on while living in the countryside. I was so thankful now to have none of that. I was content staring out the train window alone in my misery.

Riding home was a time of agonizing reflection. It stung my pride knowing that this was the course I had charted for my family. I had just finished what was probably the most expensive day of my life with how much we had invested, only to waste it. I knew a lot happen had happened, and no one would blame me, but it felt unfair: unfair to Reagan, unfair to Mai, unfair to my in-laws, and unfair to me.

I remember stopping at my in-law's house late that night on my walk home after the long train ride. They asked me how the test went, and I don't even remember what I answered. I think it was a reminder of losing Reagan for all of us. I felt like such a jerk for putting their daughter through so much, putting them through so much, and coming home a failure. They had done so much to support us, and all I had to do was pass a stupid test to make it all worthwhile and I couldn't even do that. They were kind and supportive, but there was nothing they could do to take away the feelings of shame. After a couple of minutes I left their house to walk home in the dark. I wanted the day to be over.

About a month later I received the notice that I had failed the exam. This notice was more a formality than anything.

I wondered why they even sent it. It was a final slap in the face on top of the events of the previous year, adding insult to injury. Once again, being made to feel like a complete failure came to the forefront. We had lost a precious life. I had blown our life savings. I had failed an important exam. I was unemployed. We were broke.

In the previous year, we had looked at our finances and budgeted that I would need to find employment in early February. That's how long we could last financially, but we had many big expenses with Reagan's death, and the time that we thought we had was cut short. The economy tanked, and it didn't look as if any of the opportunities I thought I had were going to work out. Everything was crashing down on us. We were getting better emotionally, but still were very fragile. Our savings were effectively gone, putting us in a very scary financial situation. The economy had fallen apart because the housing bubble burst and no one was hiring. The next best hope was for me to find a job teaching English again, but those jobs didn't start until April and we didn't have the money to get through until then, let alone afford moving to a city that might hire me. I didn't have any idea what we were going to do.

I was also burned out from being in Japan for too long. Every day was a nonstop reminder that I was American and needed to go home. Everything about Japan was starting to grate on me. Everyone was polite and friendly, but it just wasn't home. I was still devastated from losing Reagan. Mai was still struggling too. Our daughter whom we loved was so full of energy, but our spirits just weren't able to keep up with her and enjoy our time together. We started to move our belongings to my in-law's house because we had run out of money and couldn't afford the rent anymore.

By hitting rock bottom in so many areas of my life, I was finally able to let go. I was free from pretending everything was just fine. It wasn't.

Next is supposed to be the part where I tell you I did something amazing. I didn't. I wish I had a five-step program for you that fixed my life and will fix yours as well. I'd probably try to sell it on late-night cable infomercials if I did, but I don't have one. It would be great to tell you that positive thinking was the answer to all my problems. I was positive we were in trouble, and positive I didn't have a way out. My ego wished that our lives changed for the better because I did something brilliant. All my brilliant ideas left us broke and heartbroken. As a man I wish I could tell you I did something gutsy and took some big risks that paid off. All my risks left us broke. My life had completely unraveled and I was in trouble.

Having tried everything humanly possible to make something happen, I did what no self-respecting man would ever do: I surrendered. I raised the white flag and asked for mercy. I didn't understand why Reagan died. I couldn't fix that. Nothing I could do would ever bring him back. I didn't understand why we were so broke and couldn't just have things work out for us after such a tough loss. I didn't understand why I was trapped in Japan with no way out in sight. I literally had no other option but to turn to God and ask Him to take over. It was a very scary place to be. It's amazing how in our weakest hours we turn to Him, and He takes the pieces of our broken lives and builds something we never could have imagined.

Slowly but surely our luck began to change. One of my friends from college had opened a successful business and invited me to come back to the United States and work there. I was able to bring my whole family to the United States to live in a nice area and have them experience a completely different way of life. The adventure of moving to a new country was a needed change in our lives.

Coming to America and starting a new life has probably helped our emotional recovery more than we realize. I can't imagine what it would have been like to look at the city hospital where Reagan died every day. Running into my friend who was the nurse in the hospital that night again and again would have been too painful. Driving by the crematorium would have been a constant reminder of riding in the car with Reagan in his tiny coffin on my lap, and it would have hurt too much.

We're still struggling to recover financially from the time I took to study. That wiped us out completely, and my best guess is that it set us back financially ten years. Mai's been amazing about never rubbing it in my face. We both wish we had that money. There's nothing we can do about it, and in the grand scheme of things it doesn't matter. We lost someone so important to us that our other losses pale in comparison.

In contrast to our finances, spiritually I feel as if we've been catapulted forward at least ten years. When everything was going great and exactly as planned, I didn't think about God too much. I thought about Him once in a while, granted, but when everything was going well, it was always because of my hard work and the good job I was doing. Only when things really fell apart did I focus on who's really in control. As a man, it was so hard to accept that I'm not the one pulling the strings. Modern society bombards us with messages that it's all about us. We just need to get out there and take what we deserve because it's everyone for themselves. We focus on "stuff." Truth to be told I was probably among the worst. What happened to us was a great, albeit painful and tragic, reminder of what's important. The maturity and growth that came along with this hard lesson in life's realities is far more valuable than any of the money we lost along the way. I wish I could have learned these lessons and still have Reagan here today.

Now when Mai and I are facing really difficult circumstances we're able to keep things in perspective. No matter how bad things may get, we're able to take a step back and see if we're acting rationally or not. Several times I've told her that we've already been through the worst, losing Reagan. Whatever our current challenges are, they are like being on vacation compared to how tough that was. We smile at each other because we know there's more truth in that statement than not.

In closing, I want to let you know my heart goes out to you

for having the need to read this book. Going from having a pregnant wife and looking forward to a new life in the family to being sent home with a dead baby is one of the worst sucker punches in life. It's hard—really, really, hard. You can't fix it. There's no magic pill. Your wife needs you and you don't know what to do. I've walked this walk, and my best advice is to follow your heart, and surrender.

By following your heart you'll know how to help your wife. She needs you in a way that only you can fulfill. Be there for her in a way your heart tells you is right. Following your heart will let you know how to accept the acts of love that people around you will express, and how to handle the awkward moments when people don't know how to show how much they care gracefully. You'll be in tune with the feelings behind the actions people are doing for you that at first may feel strange to be able to accept.

Surrendering is against our nature as men, but that is to our own peril. It's wise, it is not weakness. What's going on in your life now is beyond your control. Let the people around you help you. You've probably heard, "Blessed are those who mourn, for they will be comforted." Surrender to God and let Him comfort you with the people in your life. There will be endless things to worry about all your life, but right now is not the time to take care of them. Let things fall where they may. You can get up and fight another day. You need to take care of yourself and your wife right now.

You are not alone. It's not your fault. There are others out there who have felt the same pain you are feeling. My prayers and many peoples' prayers are with you.

2

Why Did God Let This Happen?

This is the most gnawing question. I'm going to share with you what I believe. Please keep in mind that these are my thoughts alone. I am not a priest, pastor, or anyone specially trained. I've just been through it and here are my conclusions.

1. *God wanted us to have a stronger marriage.* You can't go through something like this without holding on to one another and loving each other more. It is times like these when your spouse is the only one who understands exactly how you feel at any given moment. Both of you are walking one of the toughest trials of life together. The bond that forms between you will grow much stronger after this painful time. Even now, years later, when we have our marital challenges I look Mai in the eyes and let her know that we've been through the worst together, losing Reagan. Since that was the hardest thing we'll ever face together, I'm sure we can overcome whatever challenges are facing us. When we catch ourselves in a bad fight over things that seem so important at the

moment, but are so unimportant in the big picture of life, I find this is a great anchor for how important we are to one another and how dedicated we need to be to each other. Our marriage needed some strength building, and this was a relationship-defining period in our marriage.

2. *God wanted us to appreciate our children as gifts.* I was guilty of taking our daughter for granted. I perceived her as another item on my responsibility list of things I had to take care of in my life. I was caught up in seeing her as a disturbance to my studies and productivity. I thought kids just "happened" and it was routine. Have sex, make baby, have baby, pay bills for the next eighteen years, and hope everything works out in the end. I was wrong. It's not that simple. Things go wrong, sometimes horribly wrong. Having Reagan taken from us showed me how precious and wonderful life is. When I see expectant mothers, I say a little prayer hoping that they get a happy ending to the pregnancy. When I see newborns, I think about how lucky those parents are, and how they probably don't even realize it. When our third child was born, I was incredibly happy. That's because I understood better after losing Reagan what a blessing having a healthy baby is and how it should be celebrated. After losing a baby, you'll never look at abortion the same way again, no matter which side of the debate you started on.

3. *God wanted us to remember what's important in life.* It's all about priorities. In our world we live in such a paradox. Every day we're told it's the car you drive, the clothes you wear, your social status that matters.

You cannot have a loss like this and not realize the insignificance of material things. The gift of life and love are the greatest gifts. We should all cherish them. As a man I never thought about them much. I always focused on producing and building my strength, finances, and influence. I never took the time to slow down and enjoy the people around me. Losing Reagan was a jolt to my value system. I'm thankful for it; I needed it. Many days I catch myself chasing things that don't really matter, but his memory reminds me of what does matter. I can think with my heart now and focus on what it's telling me to do. Your loss helps refocus you as a person. There will be things you were sure were important that will now feel like a waste of time. Small things won't bother you anymore because you will realize they're just that, small things.

4. *God is sovereign and has plans we can't begin to understand.* This was the hardest lesson for me to learn. As men we want to be in control. We want to call all the shots. We want to be the king of our domain. I had created many great plans many times only to see them fail. Many times those failures turned out to be huge blessings later down the road; I just didn't realize it at the time. Even though I'm a few years past Reagan's death, I still struggle with why he had to die. The truth is I'll probably never know or understand the reasons while I'm still on this earth. I see the spiritual growth that we've experienced and many positive developments in my relationship with Mai, my daughter, and my second son. This still doesn't tell me exactly "why" Reagan was

taken from us. Often it's hardest when we don't know the answer and don't have a way to figure it out. Coming to terms with things when that's the case is very difficult. Even when the events of life seem so wrong and there's no way something as twisted as this could possibly be His will, we need to remember it's about His plan, not ours. We need to be mature enough to accept that. He's in control, not us. This is a very hard lesson. It took me a long time to come to accept this.

5. *God gives us challenges so we can help others later when they face similar challenges.* There have been many times in my life when I've come upon hard times; it happens to all of us. It's always been the most comforting when someone has come out of the woodwork with a helping hand and a listening ear to provide wise advice right when I needed it, since they've already been down the path where I was headed. Having "been there and done that," those guides, who are really angels, have always been encouraging and helpful—and always just when I needed it the most. I hope this book has found its way into your life right when you need it. I wish I could sit down with you in person as I was able to with my friend. I wish I could cry with you and help you, but know that I am praying for you. Later on down the road, no matter how hard it is to imagine right now, you may find yourself in a position to help another dad who's going through a really hard time in his life having just lost a baby. You'll be that person in his life whom he needs at the right time.

6. *God wants us to follow Him.* With everything crashing

down around my family, I didn't have any way to save us from what was going on. It felt as if everything I thought was "for certain" was another rug getting yanked out from under us. For so long in my life I was focused on the wrong things. We were brought to the brink of despair to open our hearts to concede that we needed more than human help. Some of my favorite passages in the Bible are when Jesus tells the disciples to "Follow Me," and they drop everything and immediately follow Him. Looking back I see how ironic it was that I turned to God as the last resort out of weakness and desperation, when I should have turned to Him in the first place. He came in and through a series of events provided a better life than we had hoped. I'm not talking about the prosperity Bible. We still have our struggles in life, but His power is greater than ours. We were made weak enough to follow Him.

Mai: Even though I don't understand why Reagan died, over time I came to understand the purpose and higher meaning of his life. I became very aware that love is important. There was no running from this situation; I couldn't run away. This was something we had to do together. We had to love each other and move forward together. The Bible says love is most important, and in some crazy way this was God's way of teaching us to love one another, to love our family. All of this was a very tough lesson in love.

It was also a reminder that life is fragile. We took for

granted that we'd have a healthy baby. It's not like that. We took for granted that our daughter was born healthy. We didn't appreciate how delicate life is. Life is amazing, but we didn't have any reverence for it until Reagan died.

3

Is My Baby in Heaven?

The pastor who was kind enough to do Reagan's services was amazing. I assaulted him with my questions in search of the answer to this one question. I am too smart for my own good and really pressed him. I was as alert as I possibly could be to see if he was only telling me the things I wanted to hear. After quite a session in which we drilled deeper and deeper while he referenced scriptures, I am certain Reagan is in heaven.

When events in life come up that we can't find specific examples for in the Bible, we need to fall back on the character of God. He speaks to us through our hearts. As much as humanity relies on its intellectuals, when we set aside all the minutiae we overload our minds with to think and to take the time to feel what is around us, usually the answer is very clear. When we see things that are wrong or right, we don't need to pull out the legal code or consult lawyers. I don't need anyone to tell me when I do something wrong or right, I know. There have been countless times when my gut feeling has been the best indicator of what is the right thing to do.

Immediately following Reagan's death, I will admit that my heart meter was dysfunctional. It felt very wrong to me that he died, and I'm still not happy that he died even though I see some of the deep purpose in it now. That's why I really prodded the pastor to get the answers I was searching for and needed intellectually. Having more time pass and having grown spiritually, I've been able to remove myself from the immediate situation and shock and let my heart be my guide. It's been very hard to come to grips mentally with the fact that Reagan is in a better place even though he's not with us.

I've had the chance to meet other parents who lost children many years ago. They've shared how they miss their lost children, but are glad the ones who have passed on don't have to struggle like the ones still living do with so much of life. They share how painful it is to watch their other children grow up only to struggle with all the disappointments, sadness, and unfortunate realities that life brings. They have an interior peace knowing that some of their children's souls are already safe in heaven.

In Psalm 139 (verse 16), King David talks about how he was knit in his mother's womb and how all of his days were written in the Book of Life before he came to be, and knowing that my son Reagan couldn't have possibly done anything wrong before he was born, my heart and mind are telling me without a doubt that he's in heaven.

My heart and mind tell me Reagan is safe in heaven. I know I don't have to worry about his soul being safe. I know if he were here he'd probably have a lifetime of hardship in the ups and downs we all face. I know he's in a good place for eternity. Even though I know all this, I'm still his dad. I still love him. I still miss him. I still selfishly wish he were here.

You need to talk to someone in person who knows the scriptures much better than I do to give you the answers to all of your questions. I was nothing short of fanatical in how deep I wanted to go to get the answers. Through the questions I asked and the answers the pastor walked me through, both my intellectual questions and the doubts of my heart were satisfied. Just know that until you have that conversation, I fully believe my son Reagan is in heaven waiting to meet me and I am sure your baby is there too.

———<small>∞</small>———

Mai: Drew likes to dig deep into things, and I remember this was a big concern of his and he was determined to find the answer. He is extremely detailed and just kept digging and digging until he got closure. I'm much more spiritually oriented than intellectual, but Drew needed both. I remember he looked so relieved after talking with the pastor and being able to find where in the scriptures the pastor's answers were coming from. Your baby is in heaven waiting to meet you again.

———<small>∞</small>———

You Will See Your Baby In Heaven

4

Did This Happen Because I'm a Horrible Parent?

Assigning guilt to ourselves is such a common reaction. Please don't fall into that trap.

Looking back, there were two areas of guilt that I was trying to assign to myself as a parent: spiritual and physical.

Spiritually I caught myself looking back at the past at all the things I'd ever done. I tried to figure out which of my transgressions God was issuing punishment for, and there were plenty of sins he had to choose from. This really weighed me down for a long time because I was sure this was the sentence for some of the bad things I had done earlier in life. It was eating me up from the inside out that my son was being punished for something I did. It hurt me that Mai, who is the kindest person I know, was suffering because of my past.

None of this makes sense because as hard as it is to believe at times like this, God loves us. He is sovereign and it's about His will, not mine or yours. When I was able to take myself away as the center of the universe and see it from the perspective that God is the one orchestrating everything and it all has a much deeper meaning, it helped me to accept this. God is based on love, and because of that He only does things because He loves you. Trust me, this wasn't an easy conclusion to come to, and it will be hard to wrap your head around. Unfortunately, that's the problem. As individuals we're driven to understand everything. It's not part of our nature just to sit back and let go of control. Be patient with yourself. I lost Reagan several years ago, and others I've spoken to are decades past this, and we all agree on this point. This didn't happen because of something you did…

Assigning the blame for the way we took care of our son physically was another exercise in insanity. My wife has never smoked tobacco or anything else in her entire life, never drank more than a few sips of alcohol at a celebration (and certainly never while pregnant), and never took any kind of medication during pregnancy, and Reagan still died. Despite taking such good care of herself and Reagan, my mind was easily able to come up with every reason why we killed our baby for not being perfect parents. Mai really struggled with this one, and so did I. Many days during her pregnancy my wife had pushed herself to take our daughter out of the house so I could study. What if I hadn't been so selfish about needing to study? I thought about the time we went for a walk and I made her walk faster and farther than she had wanted to. What if I hadn't been such a jerk and made her walk that hard? The day Reagan died I had asked Mai to make me a lunch that required her to stand longer than usual. What if I had just made the lunch myself? Would Reagan still be alive? Letting your mind run wild with all the ways you possibly could have done things differently is going to happen. It's unavoidable. It's because you care. These thoughts will race through your mind, but don't blame yourself. It's not your fault.

I have asked many medical professionals, and they have assured me that sometimes these things happen. I've made my wife very uncomfortable in the rooms with doctors since our son's death because I'm not shy about going after them to get answers. I keep asking tough questions until I completely understand. I wanted to make as sure as possible that our next baby would be healthy, so I questioned, begged, and pleaded with the doctors to let me know what we might have done wrong and how we could be more responsible for the next baby. They all independently gave me the same answer: sometimes this happens; it's unexplainable, but it happens.

Your doctors will give you a report on what they think was the cause of your baby's death. If they can identify the cause of death, follow their recommendations for the future. Our report said they couldn't identify the cause, and that made us very concerned when we were considering having more children.

The point I'm trying to make is not to get caught in the trap of reflecting on every little thing you could have done that might have made a difference. It's an exercise in madness, and you'll probably never know. It's about God's plan, not about what you could have done to avoid God's plan being carried out. I've never met someone as dedicated to keeping her body pure as my wife, and Reagan still died. I can assure you it's not some wine in the pasta sauce you had at dinner a few weeks ago or anything silly like that. Set yourself free from the feelings of guilt; it's not fair to you. Ask God to give you the strength to forgive yourself.

Mai: I pointed the finger at myself for a very long time. But that's not the truth of what happened. I tried as hard as I could for so long to find a reason to place the blame on myself to justify my guilt. All the medical reasons, or lack thereof, point to the fact that I did nothing wrong during the pregnancy. It's natural for mothers to blame themselves when something happens to their babies. I suppose some people probably try to blame the doctors too. I'm convinced it's an act of God.

5

CAN I TAKE PICTURES OF MY BABY?

When Reagan was in our hospital room, I didn't know what the right thing to do was. At first I wasn't going to take a picture and thought it would be creepy to have one. Then I rationalized that even though it might not feel right at this moment, later on I would want a photo to remember him with and could delete it if I decided I didn't want it later. When I went to take a picture, Mai thought it was strange and disapproved of it, so I didn't do it.

When I did an online search for some information on stillbirth, I was quite surprised to find that people had posted many images of their lost children. Posting photos of Reagan online is not something I'd be comfortable with if I had them. I understand that everyone grieves and thinks about it differently, so I'm not condemning it; it's just not for me.

Now I wish I had a photo of Reagan next to the vase of flowers Mai keeps out in remembrance of him. A picture would help me to have a visual reminder of what he looked like and help me remember him even more than I do now. I would like to show my children the sibling they lost. Telling stories and sharing what happened verbally is one thing, but having a picture would help them understand that they really do have another brother.

If you still have the chance to take a picture, I would encourage it. That's one photo I'll never get the opportunity to retake. Even if you're not sure about it, you can always destroy it later if you have second thoughts.

———∞∞∞———

Mai: I wanted to burn Reagan's image into my memory. That's why I held him in my arms as much as I could and checked out all his hands, fingers, feet, and toes so thoroughly. It's up to the person, but as far as my opinion goes I don't regret not taking any pictures. I don't know why exactly, I think it's just my personality. I would say do what your heart is leading you to do.

———∞∞∞———

6

SHOULD I HAVE A FUNERAL?

That's a tough one. There's no right answer. We had a small prayer service for Reagan at my in-law's house with immediate family only, but it's up to you. Had this happened in the United States, I imagine we would have had a small service graveside with the same intimate group of immediate family.

Reagan was full-term, and we opted to have the local Pastor come and have a small service. He guided us in prayer and sang some hymns with us. That was plenty because we wanted to honor our son and God, but there was no way we were able to handle anyone other than the immediate family.

I'm grateful that the pastor came out and helped us do something in memory of Reagan. I don't remember much of what was said or sung, but I do remember feeling that Reagan received the proper respect that someone who had lived should have.

The idea of having anyone besides the immediate family

involved in the service was too much. We were in shock, hurting too much to pick our hearts up enough to face anyone. This had to be our close family circle only. For me, it wasn't about who was there. Mai couldn't even be there, and she was his mother. I think between the hospital and the small service at my in-law's house, everyone whom we had anticipated being a big part of Reagan's life in Japan had the chance to pay their respects.

I believe Mai and her family got what they needed in the process of saying good-bye at the hospital. It may be the way the Japanese handle death, I don't know. For me the funeral or mini-service we had was what I needed. I still don't know what it should be called officially. There's something about the ceremony of a religious man saying that this life is over on this earth that makes it really sink in for me. When the service was over, it felt as if everything were moving so fast. I was already forced to say good-bye. My only hello was holding Reagan's lifeless body in a hospital room. I wished I had taken more time to listen to him in the womb. To feel him kick. Not to have spent so much time studying, but rather to have taken at least a day to spend with Mai and Reagan while he was alive. I was his dad, and I had never taken a day to do that. I'd never get to take him camping. I'd never get to play baseball with him. I'd never have another chance to make those memories, and I had blown all the chances I had with Reagan by doing things that didn't matter anymore.

The service the pastor did placed a final marker on Reagan's life that put all of these sorrowful realizations in perspective.

It hurt, I hated having to experience it, but I needed it. That feeling of acknowledgment that his life mattered, that we cared about him very much, and that he would be missed played an important part in coming to terms with the reality of Reagan's death.

If you feel called to have a service, please don't feel you have to do it the same way we did. If your family's not feeling up to it, don't let my experience make you feel that you must. This is one of those areas where it can go either way, so follow your heart.

Mai: I'm glad we had the service. It was small and I couldn't attend, but having prayers said and some hymns sung in Reagan's memory was not only about all we could handle logistically and emotionally, but also gave me the feeling that we did the right thing for our son.

YOU WILL SEE YOUR BABY IN HEAVEN

7

How Long Will I Feel Like a Failure?

I know the feeling you're talking about. The word *failure* doesn't come close to describing how empty you feel inside. It took us a whole month after returning from the hospital to feel that we might want to get in the car and have a change of scenery, even at the risk of possibly seeing someone we knew. In retrospect we weren't quite ready even then, but we went ahead with our lives anyway. After that it took another two or three months before we started feeling that we were having normal days again.

That is not to say that you can expect all day, every day, to be the hell you're in right now. Through prayer and reading the scriptures, slowly but surely glimmers of hope were able to come into our world. We went from having a couple of good minutes here and there, to a couple of hours, to some half days, and so on. It's a gradual process that takes time, but with prayer and God's help you can make those small steps forward.

It's going to be difficult to see pregnant mothers for a long time. Newborns and babies are going to be very difficult to look at without choking up. For quite a while after Reagan was taken from us, whenever I saw a mother holding a sleeping newborn, I always thought about when I held him in the hospital and wished he would just wake up. Much like always getting asked "Where's your baby?" when you least expect it, this was one of those unexpected things that happened a lot and was challenging to deal with. These feelings of heartbreak every time we saw a newborn lasted for about a year.

All of these innocent people are going to be living reminders of your painful loss. I don't have any great advice on how to handle these situations. If you know there's an upcoming event where there are going to be a bunch of babies, or if one of your friends has a new baby, take the pressure off yourself and don't go if you're not ready. No one is going to be offended, and everyone will understand.

—◦◦◦—

Mai: I think we were able to get it together faster than most. Drew was unemployed, so we were able to spend a lot of time together and lift each other up. That may be a luxury many others don't have, but it helped us heal faster than we would have otherwise.

It took one month of solitude for me and about three months total until I was able to have anything close to a normal day. Drew was by my side all the time, and I feel that really played a huge role in how quickly I was able to recover. If the husband has to work during this time, it might take much longer. If you can be together, it would be much better.

Once I understood there was a higher purpose in Reagan's death, it helped me move along in the healing process. It took time to get there. Once my heart was in the right place, it was easier to move forward. While it was easier, it was not easy.

YOU WILL SEE YOUR BABY IN HEAVEN

8

Will I Ever Be Able to Live Normally Again?

That's a loaded question. If life were that simple, I would give you the easy yes or no answer. Life isn't like that. Life is an evolving process. What you're really asking is: Will I ever be as I was before? No, but you'll be better. Right now that's probably very hard to believe. Let me explain.

To be able to live normally, you'd have to be the same person you were before this happened. You'll never be the same again. As painful as it is now to imagine, you are going to come out of this a better person. You're going to be able to love better, show more compassion, and not let little things bother you because you will have known one of the greatest pains. So, the question becomes: Are you going to live like what you thought was normal again? No, but you will live in a better way. It's going to take a while, but you'll get there.

As a guy I know it's tempting just to say, "I'm fine," and move on. Some of the best advice I ever received on the subject of grieving was from a hospice social worker who helped my family when my dad passed away. She let me know that I'd be eligible for grief counseling if I were interested. I told her I thought I'd be able to make it on my own. Her response was, "Well, if a couple of months go by and you're not where you want to be, then give us a call and we can help you." This isn't a race to stop grieving or get over things faster than others. If you think you need to get some help, then please do so immediately. There's no shame in it, and it doesn't mean you're not a man if you do. Waiting will only make things worse for you, your wife, and everyone else in your life. If not for yourself, do it for the people you love who are counting on you.

Please understand that I'm not a professional grief counselor or an expert on the subject. There are phases to the grieving process. If you're interested in knowing what the stages of grief look like, do an online search for "grief life cycle" and you'll find a model. They come in various levels of detail, and sometimes it's hard to know exactly where you are in the process. Plus, not everyone progresses linearly through the stages; it's not uncommon for people to bounce around between some of the different stages in the cycle. The grief life cycles that are found online and created by experts look a lot different from what I've outlined here, but for us the progression seemed to go like this:

1. *Public attention faded.* People stopped asking us, "Where's the baby?" When they asked that, it felt like a knife in our hearts to have to explain Reagan's loss over

and over again. I was so relieved when that stopped happening so often. Eventually our friends stopped hiding their newborn babies from us. It was painful to see all the "little people" after we lost our little man, but it was part of people treating us as they had before Reagan died.

2. *Calendar watching ended.* I stopped counting how many days, weeks, and months old Reagan would have been if he had lived. While we were mourning, time felt as if it had stopped, and everything moved so slowly through those extremely difficult times. I couldn't help but look at the calendar and think, "Reagan's been dead for eight days, but it feels like months." As we started making progress toward living normally again, time started to speed up. They say time flies when you're having fun for a reason. The inverse is also true, and you're probably feeling that right now. The more horrible you feel, the slower things seem to go. As you start feeling better, time will speed up again.

3. *Fear was overcome.* I'm scared of a lot of things. I am fearful of scary movies, and I am scared of the dark. It's embarrassing as an adult to admit this, but the kind of fear I'm talking about is different. It's the fear that your child's death really is your fault. It's the fear that there's something fatally wrong with you. It's the fear that more bad things are going to happen to you and you can't do anything about it. It's the fear that you're going to be haunted by the memories of your lost baby. It's the fear that your spouse is going to hate you for what happened. I certainly felt these things, and I could see them affecting

Mai. In a crazy way, watching her struggle helped cure me of these fears. I saw Mai so worried and concerned about so many things that were in no way her fault. I saw her beat herself up, and if it hadn't been so real to her, then it would have been comical. Watching that helped me overcome my fears. Remember, it's not your fault and you're not to blame.

4. *Acceptance.* Of all of the high-level stages of grief, this is the one that took the most time to get to and also get through. We knew what happened; it wasn't that we were in denial until suddenly one day we just "accepted" Reagan's death. Somehow working through all the painful events—running into people with new babies, answering people who asked us where our baby was, and every other painful thing that rubbed more salt in our wound—drove Reagan's death home in our hearts more and more. Eventually his memory became who we were at a deeper level than just grieving parents. Now when we hear of people going through a similar loss, we're able to show them love and compassion without wallowing in our own misery. It took us quite a while to get here. That doesn't mean we don't remember, but we are able to show genuine empathy and not keep the focus on ourselves and our loss.

Mai: *After three months, I was able to go shopping at regular times when the store was busy and meet with my very close friends. I was able to drop off our daughter at day care and pick her up. Until then it was too hard to run into people at the store. I didn't know what to say to my friends. I couldn't to face the other moms dropping off their kids off at my daughter's day care and not look away.*

Around that same time, I was able to talk to people on the street. If anyone asked about Reagan, I could answer them without it taking all my emotional energy not to break down and cry. It still stung very badly, but I could get through it.

It still hurt to see other pregnant women and other newborns. Every time I saw a child who was the age Reagan would have been, it destroyed me on the inside. I always teared up and had to walk away. I couldn't handle being exposed to that heartache for quite a while. The wound in my heart from losing Reagan took a long, long time to heal. Now there's a really big scar that will never completely go away.

You Will See Your Baby In Heaven

9

WILL PEOPLE UNDERSTAND THAT
I WANT TO BE LEFT ALONE?

The irony here is that everyone you know is probably hoping more than anything else not to run into you. They have no idea what to say. They care, but don't know what to do. They're all imagining the worst. They're imagining the two of you in a pitch-dark room sobbing nonstop and wailing for weeks on end. That, or they're imagining you're both contemplating suicide out of guilt and taking turns talking one another down from the roof. It sounds ridiculous, but that's the way the human mind works. They're thinking the worst. This is probably a case of both sides not knowing what to say or do, but trust me: your friends and acquaintances don't want to see you just as much as you don't want to see them, but for all well-intentioned reasons.

Bosses, coworkers, friends, and family members will all help you through this incredibly difficult time. I can speak from experience that even people whom you thought had no hearts will turn into some of the most supportive people you can imagine. Yes, they will understand you want to be left alone.

A common worry is that a job will be at risk. People feel that pressing needs at the office or in some other group must be met, and if they are not the whole world will come crashing to an end. That is simply not true. Take the pressure off yourself and communicate to these people what has happened, and let them help you.

I've heard stories in which everyone in the office took the initiative to redistribute workloads, previously heartless bosses worked later for extended periods to help, and straight-commission salespeople were given draws against future earnings during these times of grief. All of this support is God showing His love through the spirit of the people around you.

You're probably not feeling up to calling everyone you know one by one and telling them what happened. I'd suggest the mass e-mail approach; "mass" doesn't mean everyone in your e-mail contact list, but figure out who really needs to know and e-mail them all at once. Don't worry about the message— short and simple works. If you can delegate this task to a close family member, that would be best.

Here's an example e-mail:

> Hello, Everyone,
>
> (Wife's name) and I just lost our baby. We are very upset and would appreciate your respecting

our privacy during our mourning. We take our commitments very seriously, and when we are feeling up to it, we plan on returning to our normal lives. We're just not there yet and don't think we'll be there for some time.

(Trusted family member's name or close friend's name who will be taking care of your affairs) will be handling all our contact with the outside world while we're taking the time we need. *(He/she)* can be reached for urgent matters at *(e-mail address)* or 000-000-0000.

We deeply appreciate your understanding and prayers,

(Your name)

YOU WILL SEE YOUR BABY IN HEAVEN

10

How Can I Best Support My Wife?

This is one of those times where just being there for one another is very important. It's also one of those times where just being there is about all you can do and is all you need to do. Add hugs and a listening ear to your presence, and you've got all the tools to be the husband your wife needs.

If you find yourselves blaming one another for what happened, I'd suggest getting some help as soon as possible. This person could be a pastor or a professional counselor, but you need to find someone qualified in this area before the situation spirals out of control. Wondering whether there was something you could have done differently is natural, but if you find yourselves pointing the finger at one another, get help immediately.

If time passes and you still feel that you need some help, don't be shy about getting it. I didn't feel the need for it, but my wife did. Looking back I should have supported her in getting that help sooner, but I was foolish. Don't make the same mistake I did. The longer you wait to get help, the bigger and uglier the problem gets, when it really doesn't have to be that way. Even though I didn't feel I needed outside help, it would have been wise to offer to go with Mai. Even if she didn't need me to go, it would have been a helpful gesture of support.

Mai seems to think I did an excellent job of being a supportive husband during this time. I wish I knew the exact recipe of what I did so I could share it with you. All I know is she didn't want to be left alone and I needed a distraction, so I brought the laptop in our room and let my mind wander while looking at news articles online. I say "looking" because I wasn't really reading, just looking at the screen and letting my mind wander as I tried to process all the events that had happened. She had had a C-section so I did tend to her physical needs, but it's not as though I were some kind of hero. I didn't have any answers. I didn't have any solutions. I was just there. Maybe that's the secret: just being there. It's a good thing that worked because at the time that's all I had to give.

Mai: Just being there is what I really needed from Drew. I didn't want to be alone; I was so scared of being alone. Drew sat next to me in the room with his computer. There were many days when it seemed as if we didn't say anything. He didn't need to say anything. I just needed him there with me. I didn't need anything special. No flowers, no cards, just him. All I needed was for him to hear what I had to say once in a while when I couldn't hold it in anymore and to be there for me.

My advice is never to let your wife be alone unless she really does want that. When Drew had to leave for the funeral and a couple of other times, I always had someone stay with me and that was extremely important. Don't let anyone you know be alone during this period of time at all. Husbands are best, but always having someone there really mattered to me. I was so scared of where my thoughts would go if I were left alone.

You Will See Your Baby In Heaven

11

WHAT SHOULD I SAY TO PARENTS WHO HAVE LOST THEIR BABY?

Reflecting back on what people said to me, I distinctly remember a few interactions. I'm going to share them, and that will help explain my answer to this question. These are other interactions besides the "How's your baby?" question that always seemed to smack us in the face when we least expected it.

While Mai was still in the hospital, I had to go out to the car for something. While I was out of the room, I decided I'd take in some fresh air and grab some things she needed from the pharmacy located across the street. This turned out to be a big mistake.

One of my older friends pulled up on a scooter and told me she was getting divorced and was very happy about it. I used to hang out at her house with her and her husband and liked them both very much. The fact that their marriage was in trouble was a surprise to me, let alone that they were getting a divorce. I just didn't know what to say. She started telling me how happy she was and how glad to be done with him. Not wanting to be rude, yet not wanting to hear this, and figuring she'd know what happened soon enough anyway, I told her we lost Reagan. I thought it would be the easy way out of the conversation and I could get back up to the hospital room with Mai. No such luck. She proceeded to tell me how it was nothing to worry about, we could still make another baby, and that her husband had knocked up some other woman and given that woman money to get an abortion while she was at home raising the kids, and on and on. She has always been one of the kindest and sweetest people. This was such a different person from the one I had known that I didn't know what to do. She was probably going through a lot too and needed to blow off some steam, and I happened to be there. I don't know how I ended that conversation, but I was completely dumbfounded. I learned my lesson about going outside during the hustle and bustle of the day when everyone is out.

Another day while we were still in the hospital, one of the teachers I used to work with started sending me messages that he had gone to Osaka and brought back a gift for me. This is a very common Japanese custom. He sent me several messages that he had driven up from his home, about an hour away, to drop off the gift. I didn't want to be rude and couldn't figure out an easy way to get out of meeting him. Japanese people can be very persistent, and appearing rude is a faux pas in their society, so I found myself painted in a corner. I ended up meeting him in front of the main entrance of the hospital, and I don't remember exactly how the conversation went.

Since he was one of teachers I had become closest to, I shared what happened, and he continued along as if everything were perfectly normal. I don't know what I was expecting, but it was weird to just keep talking as if I had told him I ate sushi for lunch.

I remember when Mai was discharged from the hospital. Going up to the nurses' station to turn in the necessary paperwork was awkward. We didn't feel any anger toward them about the situation, and I truly appreciated how hard they had worked to go the extra mile and then some for Mai and me. However, the nurse helping me would not look at me and kept her eyes down the whole time. Even though I tried to give my best thank-you, it just didn't work. She was way too uncomfortable, and my thanking her was only making her even more uncomfortable. Finally I gave up and left with the conversation hanging.

One of our close friends rents a house across the street from my in-law's house. The day we returned from the hospital, he got home while I was still unpacking the car. He was the first of our friends in our tight-knit group that I ran into. He said something in Japanese that's hard to translate, but it's comparable to "I'm sorry." I froze and didn't say anything. I didn't know how to respond. I think he understood and bowed solemnly, turned, and walked inside. I felt awful about responding to a friend in that way, but I was at a total loss for words.

My insurance agent was also a family friend whom I hung out

with many times. He was a volunteer firefighting captain and used to let me ride around with them on the fire engine and spray the fire hose. That poor guy had to come over shortly after we returned from the hospital to help us with some of the required insurance paperwork. I saw his car pull up through a crack in the blinds in our window. I could tell this was not on the list of places he wanted to be that morning, and I don't blame him. He came in and usually we would hang out for a couple of hours, but it was uncomfortable for everyone. To his credit, he was professional and caring at the same time. Usually he's a little goofy and a lot of fun to be around, but that day he had a long face and worked quickly and efficiently. He never made us feel rushed, but it was the shortest visit he'd ever paid to our home.

The reason why I share these stories is because they're the only ones I remember. I don't remember who gave me a hug or didn't. I don't remember who offered to help me or who just said, "I'm sorry." Other than these people, I don't remember anyone with whom it was awkward for ten seconds or ten minutes.

Everyone who meets a couple for the first time after a stillbirth is going to have awkward moments. There's no way around it. If you say something stupid, don't beat yourself up about it. No one knows what to say. My advice is to keep it classy, use common sense, and don't drag it out. Don't ask the mom if she knows just when the baby died or anything like that. I can't imagine anyone would, but there really is nothing good to say. Just remember the first time you meet that couple it's going to be awkward, but after that initial awkwardness, the next time you meet them you will have a much more comfortable exchange. Also, don't bring up the death as a topic of discussion unless they do. Say some kind words of condolence, and then move the conversation to another topic as quickly and gracefully as you can. If they feel like discussing the death with you that's their business, but this is certainly not the time to be nosey and pry.

If I had to recommend something to say for people you spend personal time with such as close friends and family, it would be this:

> "I heard about your loss. I'm so sorry. If there's anything I can do to help, just let me know. There's no rush, but when you and (*wife's/husband's name*) are feeling up to being social again, we'd like to (*go to dinner/get some coffee/have you over, etc.*) and in the meantime you're in our prayers."

For people you don't know quite as well, I would keep it as simple and thoughtful as possible:

> "I heard about your loss. I'm so sorry. If there's anything I can do to help, feel free to ask."

YOU WILL SEE YOUR BABY IN HEAVEN

12

How Can I Help Someone Going Through This?

Reflecting back on the greatest areas of help we received makes it easy to suggest some ways you can help that person you care about.

First, you need to ask yourself if you are very close to the grieving couple or not. By this I mean both physically and emotionally. If the answer to both is yes, then you've got a chance to be a big blessing in their lives. If not, you can skip the next paragraph and find some suggestions that will make more sense for you.

Mai's mother has an extremely close relationship with Mai and also lived a three-minute drive from our house, so she was able to be our main point of contact for everything related to the outside world. She took charge of anything and everything that came up. She did three key things for us:

1. She took our daughter off our hands and watched her for a whole month.

2. She took care of all the finances. We were able to repay

her once we were further along in the grieving process and able to think about those things again.

3. She made all the arrangements that needed to be made, no matter how big or small.

My mother-in-law is a housewife whose children have all grown up, so she had a more flexible schedule than most working people have. She was willing and able to help in the way she did. If you find yourself in a position where you have someone very close to you who needs help and you have the ability to help them, I would strongly encourage you to do it. You will not regret it, and the people you help will always be grateful for what you did.

For everyone else who wants to help but is not both emotionally and/or physically close to the grieving couple, I have the following suggestion: If they have other kids, try to find a way to help out with them.

This can be tricky because it depends on how much the kids understand about what's going on. At twenty months my daughter was clueless, so any playtime anywhere was fun. If the kids are older and understand what's going on, you'll have to use your judgment and make that call, or ask the family for their preference.

A list of other ways that you can help follows, and any of them would be appreciated.

Sympathy Cards with Cash

Money always helps, and it takes the guesswork out of what the people need. It doesn't have to be a lot of money; we received several cards with between $20 and $50. Those amounts didn't feel cheap or too much; all was appreciated.

Online Gift Cards

Gift cards might actually be better than cash. In today's world you can get anything from Amazon or a similar site, so these cards are like cash but you can spend them immediately online without actually having to go to the store. The same range of amounts listed above would go a long way toward saving the grieving couple a trip out to the store when they'd much rather stay at home and mourn.

Meal and/or Grocery Drop-offs

You do not have to commit to providing meals as often as my mother-in-law did to be helpful. Even if you can only do it once, it will mean a lot. My mother-in-law cooked all our meals and my sister-in-law dropped all of them off. It was great for a number of reasons. First and foremost, our hearts were not into doing anything, and we would not have taken the time to eat properly. There's nothing like a home-cooked meal. Second, we were not up for going out of the house at all. That small emotional effort it takes to go to the store and smile back at people who smile at you was too much for us. If you can remove that burden by dropping off meals or groceries for the couple you care about it, it would go a long way. I suggest dropping off your gift at the front door with a little note letting them know they can leave the dishes or Tupperware outside, and you'll pick them up later. This way the couple can still be with each other in that much-needed private time and yet benefit from your kindness. Even if you don't have the time to cook but you can buy something to drop off, that's just as helpful, and they'll appreciate it as much as a home-cooked meal.

Laundry

In addition to the meal drop-offs, my mother-in-law did our laundry too. I can't remember what the reasons were, but I think it was a combination of my wife having had a C-section, our mourning, and our washing machine being finicky. Regardless of the reasoning, if you are a family member and you've got the time, this is a way to help. I'd recommend any of the above suggestions first, and this could be icing on the cake if you've already committed to doing meal drop-offs. I will warn you that it's a lot of work, but the people you care about are probably wearing comfortable clothes and lying around the house. It's not as if there will be suits and pants that need pressing, so it's not the same amount of washing a couple would normally generate.

Prayer

Last, but not least, pray. Keep that family in your heart and mind and ask God to help them.

Mai: *I just wanted to be left alone. I didn't want anyone to visit, and just needed to have time with Drew. Leaving the grieving couple alone as much as possible is probably best. I'd suggest doing the acts of kindness above without forcing the recipients to answer the door and talk with you. They know you care, and this is one of those times when your actions speak louder than any words you could possibly say.*

The food was extremely helpful, and I'm very grateful for the hard work my mother and sister did in making that happen for a whole month.

Taking our daughter and watching her was the help we desperately needed the most. Having had a C-section, I was unable to pick her up and play with her in the way that she wanted and needed. More than just physically, emotionally my heart was not ready for her. I still loved her and actually cared for her even more after our son's death, but seeing any small child was hard. The guilt I was feeling was too much for me to be a mother of any kind.

I'm so thankful to my mother for giving so much of herself to support us. She did so much for us, and also for our daughter. My daughter had a blast visiting Grandma and Grandpa and had no idea anything was wrong. My mom not only saved us, but made sure my daughter was taken care of too. It took a lot out of my mom, but I'm so grateful to her for everything she did.

YOU WILL SEE YOUR BABY IN HEAVEN

13

What Should I Do with the Baby Items?

We had a room set up as a nursery with everything Reagan could possibly need, diapers and all. We were ready for our son to come into our home. We had received so many baby gifts. I knew it would really hurt Mai to see the nursery, so I threw away all the soft items such as diapers and put the rest of it out of sight in the closet.

Initially, my intention was to keep the things hidden from Mai and make a decision on what to do with them later. I probably would have left them in hiding until we decided if we would have more children, but we ended up moving back to the United States There was no point in paying to ship these items when we knew we could buy them new in the U.S. for less than what it would cost to ship them, so I decided to give them away. Many people we offered the things to didn't know what to say. They found a polite way to turn down a room full of baby items even though I knew they really needed them. Looking back, I should have realized how uncomfortable I was making people by offering them these things and just donated the goods to charity right away. It hurt us every time we opened the closet door and looked at them, and no one who knew us wanted anything to do with anything associated with Reagan's memory.

Finally, one of my good friends who was much older came to pick up our baby stuff for his daughter who was going to have a baby. This was an awkward meeting because my friend didn't really know what to say and neither did I. He couldn't ask if our baby liked the toys or anything like that, and I still didn't feel well enough to talk about pregnant women and babies, even though I was giving him an entire nursery. The understanding I received later is that his daughter didn't know where the stuff came from, and that's probably for the best. The situation is uncomfortable for everyone involved on the giving and receiving ends. After my friend left, I was kicking myself for not finding a local charity to donate the stuff to instead of putting myself through more painful moments than I needed to regarding Reagan's death.

If you choose to give the stuff away, I suggest donating the goods to the Salvation Army or a charity of your choice. My advice is to spare yourself and your friends the stress of the situation and give the items away in such a manner that the next person who receives them has no idea of the pain associated with them. You'll avoid the unpleasant handoff of the items. You'll help the next couple find a deal on things for their baby and help build the joy of pregnancy for them. They'll come across the things you've donated and be happy at their great luck in finding these brand-new items at the recycle shop. They'll be excited by their good fortune. That's the most you can hope for from these things.

The other option is to keep everything. Every time I looked at the things it hurt, so I don't think I could have used them for our next child. Just because that's the way I felt doesn't mean you have to do it the same way. I hung onto almost all of the items because we had spent so much money on them and we were broke.

The question really comes down to, is it worth holding on to these things and saving the money so that you can use them if you have another child? If the memories associated with the items are painful enough to answer no, donate them. If the answer is yes, then keep them. Be sure to include your wife in this decision; her input is critical.

YOU WILL SEE YOUR BABY IN HEAVEN

14

When Will We Have Sex Again?

Very few things in life take away the urge for intercourse like this situation. I'm not a professional, so the best I can do is to share our story. For us, we returned to intimacy right around the time my wife was medically cleared for sex post C-section. I think men get to the point of desire and ability to engage in sexual activity much more quickly than women.

For the first couple of months, whenever we had sex I struggled with knowing that my dead baby had been "in there." It was a strange feeling to be getting so much pleasure from a place where such a horrible thing had happened. The fresh scar on my wife's belly that I saw every time I took off her clothes reminded me time and time again. There was no pretending even for a moment that a dead baby hadn't been pulled from her when I saw that scar.

I felt like such a jerk for needing this kind of comfort from my wife. I had urges and needs, and they didn't always come at the most opportune times. I could tell Mai was letting me do the things I wanted to do to help me feel better. Her heart wasn't in it, and at the same time I needed it. For a while I had guilty feelings of selfishness after sex.

The thoughts of Reagan having died in my wife's womb faded over the course of the following year and rarely, if ever, came back. Ever since the time that Mai became pregnant with our third child, I've never had that thought again.

It did take some time for me to come to grips with the crazy dynamic that my wife's body could bring so much pleasure as well as pain and have that knowledge no longer produce any negative thoughts or memories. If you find yourself where I was—struggling with the desires you have versus wanting to restrain yourself from asking this from your wife—I'd say you're probably normal. Give it time, and once all hearts are healed, things will feel right again.

As for the female side of things, it's a lot harder to say because I'm a man. Mai was very concerned about becoming pregnant again too quickly. Getting pregnant post C-section is not recommended for at least a year and a half, according to Japanese doctors, but a large part of it was giving her the time she needed to recover emotionally. That emotional healing needed to happen in two parts. First and foremost was coming to terms with what had happened. Second was to be ready to trust the Lord, to try again, and to have faith that we could have another child. I'm sure if it had been entirely up to Mai, having sex after Reagan died would have been a lot further along in her emotional healing process.

———✦———

Mai: *Because of the C-section we were not allowed to have intercourse for the first month. I know Drew really wanted to have sex, so we did at the one-month mark. That's probably normal for the husband to want it, but it did take me a while before I had sex because I wanted to, as opposed to my husband's desire for intimacy. How much of that fear was about not wanting to get pregnant again because of the C-section, as opposed to not wanting to have sex because Reagan died, is really hard to remember now. I remember the fear I felt and that it took a long time to get over it.*

———✦———

YOU WILL SEE YOUR BABY IN HEAVEN

15

What About Having More Children?

We have had another child since losing Reagan. He is a healthy, happy bundle of joy. Having another baby after a stillborn baby is stressful. It is also one of the most amazing feelings in the world.

We made it a priority to pray every day during the next pregnancy. I don't know what milestones other couples put out there for feeling better. For us, having a healthy baby in our arms at the hospital was the only thing that was going to bring us relief. That was the finish line. We prayed for that every day, sometimes several times a day, and God answered our prayers. Without our faith and God's love, I don't know how we would have managed the stress and uncertainty of the next pregnancy.

I don't want to make it sound as if we sat at home and chewed our fingernails and were on edge every single day because it wasn't like that at all. We had a lot of great family time together, did many fun things, and enjoyed life while Mai was pregnant. There were some mornings when she was worried about what might happen. We used those times, as well as the good times, as prayer opportunities to ask God for His help. Through His loving hands we were supported in both happy and stressful times until our next baby was delivered safely into our arms.

Your wife and baby will have to have many more checkups the next time around. It will be deemed a high-risk pregnancy. I won't go into detail about what tests and how often, but know that the medical staff will be there to take extra special care of your wife and to ensure as much as they can that nothing goes wrong.

Knowing the pain you're feeling now, I can assure you there are no words to describe the feeling you will have when your next baby is born. My daughter was born first, and becoming a new dad was incredible. When our third child was born safe and sound, the relief, joy, and happiness was a different incredible feeling. Both could easily be described as the best days of my life, but the emotions were not the same.

I love my second son more freely than I otherwise would have had we not lost Reagan. I feel more deeply what a blessing a healthy baby is and how lucky I am to have had two of them who are still with me. My daughter was our first child, and I took it for granted that babies are born healthy. The idea that any result other than a healthy baby could happen when a woman was pregnant had never entered my mind.

If you're medically cleared to have children in the future, I recommend you pray about it. I honestly didn't think I'd be up for the emotional roller coaster ride, but now I'm happy we did it. My heart loves more deeply now than it ever could have hoped to before.

Mai: After Reagan died, I didn't think I could handle being pregnant again. Every time I thought about carrying another child, it was scary; I didn't have the confidence I could carry another baby, or if I did that the child would live. I knew I wouldn't be able to handle another lost baby. I also questioned if I would have the energy and will to raise another child after feeling so drained from Reagan's death.

It took about two years before I felt I wanted another child. After two years I thought it would be a good idea for our daughter to have a sibling. The two-year mark was also about how long it took me to stop looking at every child I passed who was the same age Reagan would have been and not fight back tears. Even after those two years I was always fearful of pregnancy, but wanting to make a sibling for our daughter was stronger than the fear. I was scared, but I knew it was important, so we conceived another child.

Now that our second son has been born healthy, I'm very happy. The doctors took really good care of us and checked up on him many, many times during the pregnancy. We had since moved to a large city in the United States with a nearby hospital that had all the equipment on hand to take care of our new baby in case anything happened. We had all kinds of contingency plans if something went wrong. They made me feel safe and that they could and would take great care of me and my next child.

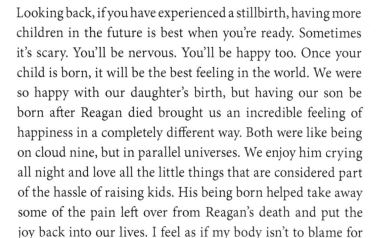

Looking back, if you have experienced a stillbirth, having more children in the future is best when you're ready. Sometimes it's scary. You'll be nervous. You'll be happy too. Once your child is born, it will be the best feeling in the world. We were so happy with our daughter's birth, but having our son be born after Reagan died brought us an incredible feeling of happiness in a completely different way. Both were like being on cloud nine, but in parallel universes. We enjoy him crying all night and love all the little things that are considered part of the hassle of raising kids. His being born helped take away some of the pain left over from Reagan's death and put the joy back into our lives. I feel as if my body isn't to blame for Reagan's death anymore.

16

How Can I Memorialize My Child?

This is a very personal decision, so I'm sharing what we did. It is by no means meant to be authoritative.

As you know, we were living in a very small town in Japan when we lost Reagan. The street where my in-laws live cuts right through the cemetery. I've never seen a city layout like it in the United States A very narrow road on which only one car at a time can pass while opposing traffic waits cuts right through the cemetery and is one of the main roads for getting across town.

To walk from my in-law's house to our son's gravesite took less than five minutes. In Japan the gravesites are really more like a group of family ashes all buried next to each other under a main gravestone. To keep it simple, think of it as every male head of household having his own gravestone with his family members (all in urns) buried with him under and around that gravestone. My father-in-law visited his family gravesite every day. It is located right on the edge of the road. When I say "edge of the road" I mean it; this is a very narrow street, even by Japanese standards, and the driver needs to pay close attention. When you drive by this gravesite, you could roll down the car window and reach out and touch the gravestone if you wanted to. My father-in-law is Buddhist, so he burns incense and prays for his family every day at the gravesite. I know he prayed for our son every day while we were in Japan and still does.

Once Mai was well enough after the C-section, we made daily trips to our son's gravestone to remember him and console each other. I remember Mai often put fresh flowers there, and we held that tradition for a while. Because of the proximity of his grave to where we were living, the lines of formally visiting the gravesite and just driving by but remembering him in our hearts were very blurred. Eventually our formal visits got to be fewer than daily, but we still drove right past his grave several times every day.

Since then we have moved to the United States and will most likely move across borders several more times in our lifetime. It didn't feel right to leave Reagan in Japan when we came to America, so we decided to take him with us. Mai wanted to get another gravestone, and I suggested we just keep him with us in our house. She wasn't a fan of that suggestion, but I got the idea from a friend's family. Their grandfather had built the house they were living in. They knew their grandfather put his life's work into that house, so they kept his ashes in the house to memorialize him.

Knowing that we were a young international couple and that we'd probably move at least six more times in our lifetime, I didn't feel that meant every time we moved we needed to buy a new gravestone and new gravesite plot. Mai reluctantly agreed.

I left Japan before the rest of my family to find an apartment for us and took Reagan's ashes with me. Be forewarned that the airlines have regulations for traveling with human remains, so be sure to look them up and stay compliant if and when you choose to do this.

Reagan's ashes are in a spot in our home in an urn with a tiny vase next to it that holds some flowers, which Mai changes every couple of days. On his birthday we get a really nice bouquet. It's probably surprising to read that I opted for this after sharing with you how I'm a wimp when it comes to corpses, but the ashes don't bother me at all. I think Mai is happier now that we have him with us in the house, even though she doesn't admit it.

Originally the plan was that when we found ourselves in a permanent home, or at least where we think we would be permanently, we would make proper arrangements to have him buried again. Now I imagine we'll keep him in our home until one of us dies, and then have him buried next to one of us. For us and where our hearts are now we feel this is the right thing to do. I imagine everyone has their own ideas and strong feelings about what to do. The last thing I want you to feel when reading this is that you have to do it the way we did.

Mai: I was raised Buddhist, so at first I went out of my way to put out flowers, snacks, and things like that for Reagan every day. It was the way I was raised and the only way I thought was right. When we first moved to the United States, I kept that up for a little while in front of his ashes inside our home. As my Christian faith grew, I still felt compelled to put out flowers for him. Now I feel it's much more important that he's remembered in my heart rather than with any treats or flowers I could put out for him.

I still want to have a proper grave for him when we figure out where we'll live permanently. My parents still visit his grave every day and put out flowers, burn incense, and leave treats for him. Even though his remains are no longer there, that's how they keep him in their hearts. Because his grave is right on the edge of a street that many elementary school kids take to school, my parents tell me that every day the little kids take the treats laid out for Reagan on their way to school. My husband and I find that funny and just one of those things in life that happens. Those children are so young they have no idea what the treats are there for, so it's cute. Really at this point it's how my parents keep him in their hearts, and if some other kids get to have a little bit of happiness from the luck of walking by when there's something laid out, then good for them.

I am looking forward to Reagan's remains having a permanent home. I want his remains to be where I can go and visit and do some of the customs honoring the dead as my parents taught me while I was growing up. Having him here with us has been good, but I feel that he needs to have a permanent internment somewhere where we'll be buried too.

YOU WILL SEE YOUR BABY IN HEAVEN

Conclusion

A Message of Hope

I understand what you're feeling right now. I've been in your shoes. My heart and prayers are with you. I wish there was some way I could undo what happened and take away all the pain you're suffering right now.

I wrote this book having been through the pain you've felt so far and the pain you're going to feel over the next couple of months and years. I'm here to tell you that as hard as it is now you're going to get through this. There is no shortcut, but on the other side of this you will come out a better person.

Mai: Your child in heaven doesn't want you to cry and be miserable. Your child knows and feels your love. God doesn't want you to be miserable. Your child is in heaven, but still wants you to pick your head up and move forward. This feels like the lowest point in your life and that you're abandoned, but really God's holding you. We are several years out and have a feeling of gratefulness from our experience, as hard as that may be for you who are reading now to believe.

———∞∞∞———

You will have some of the lowest lows anyone has ever known. You will be able to appreciate good times better than you did before. You'll be a better partner to your spouse because of this difficult walk together. You'll be a better parent to your current children and to children you may have in the future because of your appreciation of how much of a blessing they are in your life. You'll understand better how precious life is. You'll have stronger faith in God. You'll have the chance to help others in pain and walk with them in their time of need.

Your perspective on life is going to be corrected. You're going to realize what matters. You're going to see that your child's short, precious life will have had a more positive impact on your family's lives than you can possibly imagine.

Many of the most heroic and admired people in history have dedicated their whole lives to spreading this message of hope and love to even a few people. Their lives are considered some of the best lives ever lived. This wake-up call to the preciousness of life is the greatest gift one human being can give to another.

Your child has lived a life like this.
Your child has given this gift to you.
Be thankful.
You will see your baby in heaven.

Made in the USA
Lexington, KY
24 June 2013